Legal Notices

The purchaser or reader of this publication assumes complete and total responsibility for the use of this information within. While all attempts have been made to verify information provided in this publication, neither the Author nor the Publisher assumes any responsibility for errors, omissions, or contrary interpretation of the subject matter herein.

This publication is not intended for use as a source of legal or accounting advice. The Publisher wants to stress that the information contained herein may be subject to varying state and/or local laws or regulations. All users are advised to retain competent counsel to determine what state and/or local laws or regulations may apply to the user's particular situation or application of this information.

The purchaser or reader of this publication assumes complete and total responsibility for the use of these materials and information. The Author and Publisher assume no responsibility or liability whatsoever on the behalf of any purchaser or reader of these materials, or the application or non-application of the information contained herein. We do not guarantee any results you may or may not experience as a result of following the recommendations or suggestions contained herein. You must test everything for yourself.

Any perceived slights of specific people or organizations are unintentional.

Copyright © 2014 by Mok Tuck Sung
All rights reserved.
ISBN: 1505375118.
ISBN-13: 978-1505375114.

Business Owners' Guide to Better Cash Flow
By Mok Tuck Sung
Outline

1. Introduction – You Need Clarity

In this appealing, inviting opening, the author distinguishes between "managing" a business and "doing business"; the latter includes working on the operations of the business, whereas the former includes strategically growing the business.

If a business owner wants to have more cash at the end of each year, it is crucial to learn how to manage and enhance the business. Often, business owners fret over **profit and loss statements**, but either ignore or are unable to understand the importance of the **cash flow** statement of their company. *Cash is the lifeblood of any business,* so this book will help businesspeople understand their business's cash flow right from the very basics.

2. Basics of Cash Flow

This chapter supplies the basics of cash flow, the lifeblood of any business, in a fashion that is easy to understand for beginners yet enlightening for experts. This chapter explores how cash flows in a business, how to manage cash flow, and how to use cash flow management strategically to help grow the business.

3. Impact of Macro Environment on Cash Flow

A company does not exist in a vacuum and, hence, it is impacted by a number of external factors. The company needs to learn to adapt and react to external stimuli to grow and remain profitable. In this chapter, readers will learn about some of these external influences and how to cope with the changes. After reading this chapter, readers will be able to:

- ✓ Understand the impact of the external environment on cash flows
- ✓ Understand the need to realign strategies to the changing business environment

4. Cash Flow: A Quantitative Analysis

It is essential to understand the current situation and know all the metrics that could give readers a clear picture of managing cash flow in the future. This chapter discloses the information that financial statements and cash flow statements can reveal and where to find the information to evaluate critical evaluation metrics.

After reading this chapter, readers will be able to:

- ✓ Understand the components of the cash flow statement
- ✓ Understand the metrics that could be used to gauge the cash flow strength of the company
- ✓ Calculate and analyze the company's cash position using these metrics

5. Financial Drivers of Cash Flow

Any company's cash flow is driven by a number of factors, and it is important for every business owner to understand what these drivers are and how they impact a business's cash flow. This chapter will explain the seven cash flow drivers and how they impact the cash flow.

After reading this chapter, businesspeople will be able to:

- ✓ Understand the advantages of cash flow analysis and control
- ✓ Understand the components of a cash flow statement

6. Managing Cash: Inflows

This chapter will explore the importance of managing operating cash inflows and the strategies for same.

After this chapter, readers will be able to:

- ✓ Understand the impact of accounts receivables on cash flow
- ✓ Understand the importance of a shorter collection period
- ✓ Be able to use an accounts receivables' aging report to accelerate cash inflows
- ✓ Implement a cash flow-friendly credit policy
- ✓ Understand the importance of factoring

7. Managing Cash: Outflows

This chapter will discuss the other most important aspect of managing operating cash flow, which is minimizing (or delaying as much as possible) cash outflows.

After this chapter, readers will be able to:

- ✓ Understand the impact of accounts payables on cash flow
- ✓ Understand the importance of a longer creditor period
- ✓ Be able to use an accounts payables aging report
- ✓ Implement a cash flow-friendly payment policy
- ✓ Understand the importance of managing a "cash pool"

8. Optimizing Your Sales Function

The sales function needs to carry out tasks with cash flow awareness. They should know the impact of making a certain sale to a certain customer on the business's cash flow. This chapter will explore one of the most important parts of a business. Although not exactly cash focused, it has the highest impact on a business's cash flow.

This chapter will enable readers to:

- ✓ Understand the true purpose of the sales function
- ✓ Understand the objectives of the sales function to maintain a sustainable business
- ✓ Be able to understand the importance of a sales forecast
- ✓ Be able to do a basic product analysis

9. Cost Optimization: Activity-Based Costing

This chapter will explain **activity-based costing (ABC)** as a tool for cost reduction in a business. ABC does not replace the existing cost management methods in a company; rather, it is a once-off exercise. Using ABC helps management identify unnecessary or duplicated activities. It also helps in evaluating the benefit provided by the activities performed throughout the company.

This chapter will empower readers to:

- ✓ Understand what activity-based costing is
- ✓ Understand the ABC process
- ✓ Be able to understand the ABC basics to control costs

10. Cash Flow Management: Finance Function

This chapter will explain the contribution of the finance function in cash management for a small business. This chapter will cover the three main activities to be handled by the finance function, in terms of cash management, which are: **Investing**, **Financing**, and **Borrowing**.

This chapter will equip readers to:

- ✓ Understand the function of the finance division in cash management
- ✓ Understand the basics of creating a short-term investment policy
- ✓ Understand how to evaluate long-term investments
- ✓ Understand the various sources of borrowing cash in terms of a shortfall

11. Forecasting Cash Flow for Future Periods

This chapter will help readers understand the advantages of knowing expected cash flows in advance. By planning for future cash flows, the company can avoid surprises and possible crises. The primary focus of cash flow planning is to have future expected cash inflows exceed cash outflows and take essential steps to sustain positive cash flow. A comparison and analysis of planned and actual results equips businesspeople with the information necessary for well-informed decision-making and enhanced future planning.

12. Cash Flow: Analyze Actuals vs. Forecast

This chapter will discuss cash flow analysis and control, which is as important as profit analysis or cost analysis for companies in this dynamic business environment.

Readers of this chapter will be able to:

- ✓ Understand the advantages of cash flow analysis and control
- ✓ Understand the components of a cash flow statement
- ✓ Understand the use of ratio analysis for cash flow analysis.

13. Free Cash Flow and Business Value Creation

This chapter will discuss in detail the importance of **free cash flow (FCF)** and its impact on the overall business's value, also known as enterprise value.

Readers of this chapter will be able to:

- ✓ Understand the concept of FCF and business value
- ✓ Understand how FCF impacts the business's value
- ✓ Calculate the enterprise value of a business

Table of Contents

Introduction – You Need Clarity 11
Basics of Cash Flow 15
Cash Flow: A Quantitative Analysis 31
Financial Drivers of Cash Flow 41
Managing Cash: Inflows 50
Managing Cash: Outflows 63
Optimizing Your Sales Function 76
Cost Optimization: Benchmarking 89
Cost Optimization: Activity-Based Costing 100
Cash Flow Management: Finance Function 111
Forecasting Cash Flow for Future Periods 122
Cash Flow: Analyze Actuals vs Forecast 136
Free Cash Flow and Business Value Creation 146
Doing Nothing is Unacceptable 155
About the Author 157

Introduction – You Need Clarity

A business is usually started to make money. The central idea is usually to put in a small sum of money, and then generate a large sum of money from it on a regular basis. This is the dream of most business owners, but unfortunately, only a handful of business owners are able to achieve it. The majority of entrepreneurs are able to make just enough, and many fail as well.

Most small business owners learn a skill, and set up their own business when an opportunity arises. Now, most of the time, they are equipped to "do" all aspects of the business, such as running a shop or selling a product, understanding contracts, and operating the factory.

However, they fail to understand at times that "doing" business is very different from "managing" business. "Doing business" would include working on the operations of the business, whereas "managing business" includes strategically growing the business. From the perspective of the business owner, "managing" business is so much more crucial than "doing" business.

The most important aspect of managing business is managing the money generated. The flow of money and cash through the business is reported in the form of **financial statements**.

Many business owners feel that as long as they focus on the operational aspects of the business, their firm will automatically have more cash; however, this is far from the truth. If a business owner wants to have more cash at the end of each year, it is crucial to learn how to manage and enhance the business. The financial statements can give you a brief idea about your business's performance. It helps you to understand exactly where the business stands and how much cash there is in your business.

Often, business owners fret over the **profit and loss statements**, but either ignore or are unable to understand the importance of the **cash flow** statement of their company.

Cash is the lifeblood of any business.

You need cash to pay your suppliers and your employees, as well as to pay off the taxes, debts, and loans. You will also need cash to pay yourself.

All business activities can be linked back to cash. No matter how great or unique your product or service is, if you are not able to transform it into cash, the business will most likely fail sooner or later.

The formula for cash flow is very simple:

> Cash Inflow – Cash Outflow = Positive/Negative Cash

However, business owners at times find it hard to understand cash flow. In this book, we will help you understand your business's cash flow right from the very basics. You will also gain valuable tools to understand how to enhance your business's cash flow.

At the moment, we simply need to understand and remember that for most failed businesses the reason most often is not lack of profit, but lack of cash.

Many business owners don't even realize when the cash is about to run out in their business. Hence, when the cash runs out, they panic and seek short-term solutions, which are not sustainable and hurt the business even more. These typical solutions usually include:

- Reduce costs/expenses
- Reduce/stop benefits
- Reduce salaries
- Reduce prices to sell more
- Stop advertising
- Cut other marketing activities
- Buy cheaper raw materials, hurting product quality

In this book, we will help you understand first the basics of cash flow and how the cash actually flows through a business. We will discuss in detail various internal and external factors that can have an impact on your business's cash flow. We will also explain why an increase in revenue does not translate into an increase in cash.

After we understand the basics, we will move on to explaining the strategies you can use to enhance your cash inflows and reduce/delay your cash outflows. We will explain how you optimize your business's costs so that you have an optimum expenditure, which can enhance cash flow while maintaining the quality of your product or service.

We will then explain how to measure the impact of the strategies you are utilizing and also how to forecast and subsequently achieve your optimum cash flow.

The diagram below explains the road map that we will follow to create your business's value by optimizing cash flow.

Free cash flow and business value creation

Getting the cash you want
- Forecasting cash flow for future periods
- Cash flow: Analyze actuals vs forecast

Optimization for better cash flow
- Managing cash: Inflows
- Managing cash: Outflows
- Optimizing your sales function
- Cost optimization: Benchmarking
- Cost optimization: Activity-based costing
- Cash flow management: Finance function

Understanding cash flow
- Basics of cash flow
- Impact of macro environment on cash flow
- Cash flow: A quantitative analysis
- Financial drivers of cash flow

Basics of Cash Flow

We understand that cash flow is the lifeblood of any business as it is critical to sustain as well as grow the business. However, we need to understand that the scope of cash flow management is much larger than just keeping track of how much cash flow in and out of the business. By using a more strategic approach, many businesses are able to free up their cash, which could be used to invest in new products or for market development, paying back debt and for financing other strategic initiatives. A business with strong cash flow is also in a better position to negotiate better financing terms with creditors and better discounts with suppliers.

Strategic cash flow management:

The key to sustainable growth

In this book, we will try to understand the importance of strategic cash flow management and its contribution to business success. We will also discuss strategies to identify problems that are warning signals for us to have better cash flow management practices. Let us first look at how the cash flows in a business.

How does cash flow in a business?

It's essential for business owners to understand how cash flows in their business so that they can manage the flow of cash in the correct manner and direction. It is quite easy to understand the basics of cash flow that includes revenue, profits, and sales. The basics of cash flow include a few simple items. All you need to understand is that your cash inflows should be more than your cash outflows. Now the money a business earns is called **revenue** or **sales** and cash flowing out of the business is an **expense** in some form, such as rent, telephones/communications, utilities, etc. Now, your **profit** is the cash that is left after the expenses are subtracted from revenue; however, profit cannot be used to run a business. The reason is that in today's dynamic business accounting, profits and cash could be a significantly different figure due to **accrual accounting** and **sales on credit**.

Now to have any sort of control over the cash flow management of your business, you need to keep and maintain regular records of financial transactions. You could use economical accounting software for this purpose or even maintain your accounts manually; you just need to keep in mind that you need to update those records on a regular basis, preferably every day.

From those records you will get a clear idea about the amount you owe to other businesses as well as the amount you are owed along with your cash position. It is also important to keep track of your revenue and expenses along with the cash. *Successful businesses have transparency about their financial position and track it regularly.*

Now, we have understood the importance of understanding the flow of cash in your business as well as the importance of record keeping. Let us now look at how the cash actually flows in a business.

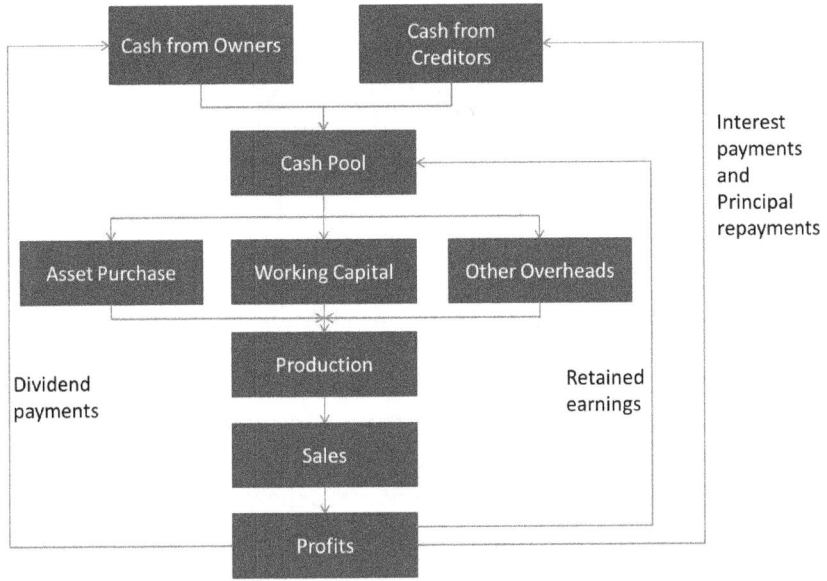

Initially, a business is started by using cash from its owners and possibly also from creditors. This cash forms the cash pool to start the business. This money is then utilized to purchase assets such as equipment, premises, etc. The cash is further used to buy raw materials, and pay salaries and other overheads. After this, production begins, resulting in the finished product, which is then sold to customers to generate revenue and, eventually, profits.

The profits are used to pay dividends to the business owners and pay back the borrowed money to the creditors. The remainder of the profits could be retained in the cash pool to invest in the company's growth.

Cash flow management

Most business owners clearly understand that their business needs to have more cash inflows than outflows. No business can grow sustainably or even survive if there are persistent cash flow troubles and there is difficulty making payments to employees and suppliers. Growth halts when a business has to forego investment or business improvement opportunities due to a lack of cash.

However, business owners are often so wrapped up in smoothly running and maintaining their day-to-day operations that they are unable to invest any time in developing a strategic cash flow management process that is likely to help them avoid cash shortages and maximize profits.

For most small businesses, the following would be a typical scenario: The business owner starts the business with his/her own savings. The business starts generating revenue and, at least initially, reinvests most of the profits back into the business. However, with this approach, despite the growth in business, several key considerations are neglected, which are critical for long-term sustainability.

These include:

- Is the cash flow being maximized: Is the business managing cash inflows as quickly as possible, and delaying cash outflows as much as possible?
- Is the business making sales to the right customers?
- Is the business able to keep costs at an optimum level?
- Is there scope to enhance the business process to improve cost effectiveness?
- What's the optimum amount of cash pool needed for your business to avoid shortfalls and keep the opportunity cost of idle cash at a minimum?
- How should the excess cash be invested?
- Is the business able to get the best possible discounts from suppliers?
- Is the business credit worthy? Can it secure funds when needed on the best possible payment terms?

After reviewing the questions in the abovementioned scenarios, the business owner or business managers might realize that to stay on a growth path, the business would need a more sophisticated approach. As the business expands, it needs:

- To evaluate its current cash position accurately and forecast the cash flow to get an idea of the cash required to meet its outflows on a regular basis;
- To optimize cash flow through both operational and investment strategies, such as putting the excess cash in the best available investment options and making sound capital expenditure decisions; and

- To analyze the quality and sustainability of sales revenue, manage cash cycles, and control costs.

Using strategic cash flow management to help grow the business

The actual implementation of a **strategic cash flow management** initiative starts from the top in *any* business. When a small business owner understands the correlation between cash flow management and corporate performance, only then are they likely to make it a priority.

The business needs to develop a systematized process to track and analyze key cash flow metrics. This would provide a performance baseline against which the business owner could measure ongoing progress. To achieve effectiveness and efficiency via strategic cash flow management, businesses must actively track and manage data about their current cash position. It is also essential to develop realistic future projections and goals.

In this book, we will discuss each and every one of the abovementioned questions in detail, enabling you to identify the problems and enhance your company's strategic advantage through cash flow management.

Impact of Macro Environment on Cash Flow

A company does not exist in a vacuum and, hence, it is impacted by a number of external factors. The company needs to learn to adapt and react to external stimuli to grow and remain profitable. In this chapter, we will learn about some of these external influences and how to cope with the changes.

After reading this chapter, you will be able to:

- ✓ Understand the impact of the external environment on cash flows
- ✓ Understand the need to realign your strategies to the changing business environment

The business environment is changing all the time. Macroeconomic factors impact a business in a number of ways, but the negative impact could be avoided by timely action. Changing macroeconomic factors have different impacts on different businesses depending on the type of product the company manufactures; however, it is universal that in trying times, the business needs to adapt or it will lose customers.

> *Differentiation is the key to gaining the competitive advantage in a highly competitive market*

Some of the main macroeconomic factors, which impact businesses, are:

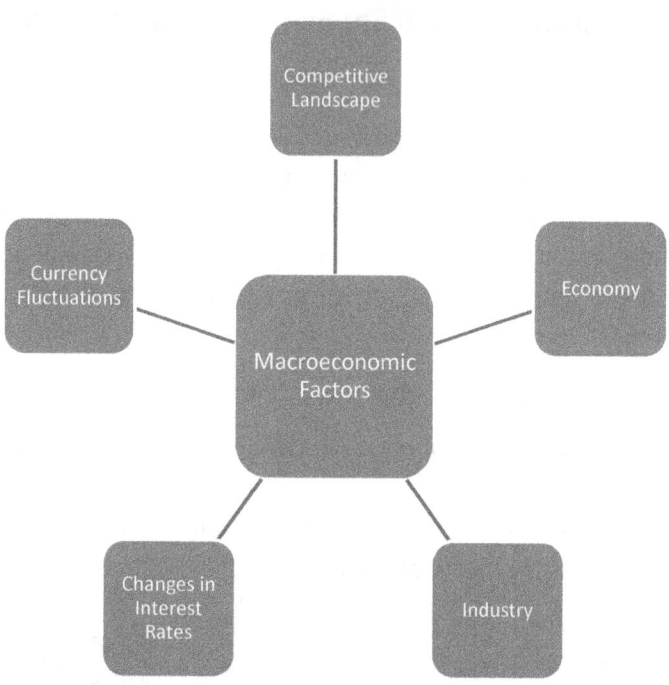

In this chapter we will discuss each of the abovementioned factors.

Competitive landscape

Competition has a very high impact on a business's revenue and profitability, in turn affecting the company's cash flow. The level of competition is dependent on the industry and market the business operates in, such as:

<u>Many rival businesses:</u> This is common for retailers and generic service providers.

<u>Few large rival companies:</u> This kind of competition is common in fast moving consumer goods manufacturers, such as Coke and Pepsi.

<u>Rapidly changing competitive environment:</u> This kind of competitive environment is usually common for companies that are highly dependent on technology. An example of this would be mobile phone manufacturers.

A business needs to be aware of its competition and competitive environment so that it is able to react to an increase in competition, such as a new promotion offered by a competitor or a new product launch. To survive in a competitive environment, a business needs to differentiate its products and services. The most commonly used strategies to tackle competitive pressure are:

- Product price reductions
- Enhanced quality
- Increases expenditure on promotion/advertising
- Cost reductions

Economy

Economic situations usually impact all businesses, but most of the time, small businesses feel the impact of economic changes more profoundly than their larger counterparts. An economic upturn usually provides a surge in business opportunities, whereas a downturn can have a severe negative and lasting impact.

Strong economy positively impacts most businesses

Impact of economic upturn

In general, a strong economy translates into greater prosperity for all businesses. As disposable income increases, consumer confidence grows, prompting the purchase of essential and non-essential goods. This encourages further growth as money is pumped back into the economy. However, small businesses need to be careful as an economic upturn can often lead to business expansion due to growing demand, which if not properly planned could lead to disaster if the economy starts to falter. For instance, let's take an example of a retailer. He hires additional employees and buys another warehouse to cater to the increasing demand. Now, if the economy starts taking a downturn, the same decisions could have a huge negative impact on the company's cash flow. Hence, it is necessary to make expansion decisions after careful analysis.

Impact of a slow economy

In general, an economic slowdown brings a plethora of challenges for small businesses. As the consumer's disposable income decreases, they are more likely to be much more careful with their expenditures, which translates into decreased revenue for small business owners. A declining stream of profit can make it challenging for a small business to repay creditors, which in turn is likely to negatively impact its long-term relationship. A company facing financial crisis is much less likely to qualify for loans for capital expenditures and working capital, which could limit the company's growth opportunities.

However, small businesses, which have substantial financial backing, could benefit from an economic downturn as they get the opportunity to expand by acquiring struggling competitors or gaining customer bases of out-of-business competitors.

Adapting to the economic environment

Small companies have an advantage over large companies when it comes to adapting to changes in the economy. Generally, small businesses are likely to have an easier decision-making process compared to large companies who need to call stockholder meetings to change business strategy and direction. Thus, a small business can rapidly adjust to a changing economy by making quick decisions about reducing costs by decreasing the workforce, enhancing product offerings, or rebranding the company if needed.

Industry

Industry is another factor, which significantly impacts a company and its cash flow. Let us discuss these with the help of *Porter's five forces model.*

Threat of new entrants	• If it is easy for new companies to enter the business, the industry will be more competitive due to the number of competitors. A highly competitive industry makes it difficult to grow and increase revenues, directly impacting the business cash flow. Factors that are likely to reduce the threat of new entrants are called barriers to entry, such as loyalty to major brands, high fixed costs, and government regulations.
Bargaining power of suppliers	• This indicates the level of pressure suppliers can put on a business. If the number of suppliers in the market is low and there is no substitute, it enhances the bargaining power of suppliers. The suppliers with high power can impact a company's margins and volumes.
Bargaining power of buyers	• This indicates the level of pressure buyers can put on a business. If the number of buyers in the market is low and if a buyer purchases large volumes of product, then it increases the bargaining power of buyers. However, if a company produces a product that has no substitute, it reduces the bargaining power of buyers. The buyers with high power can impact a company's margins and volumes.
Availability of substitutes	• This indicates the likelihood that customers will switch to a competitor's product or service. If the cost of switching is low, then it could be a serious threat.
Competitive rivalry	• This indicates the intensity of competition within an industry. If an industry is highly competitive, then generally, it is likely to earn low returns because of the high cost of competition.

Changes in interest rates

The primary method to control inflationary pressure on an economy is controlling the interest rates. Hence, we hear about interest rate fluctuations often. These changes in interest rates have a number of different effects on businesses.

Effects of an increase in interest rates include:

<u>Higher debt repayment costs</u>: Most businesses have debt for both long-term investments and short-term needs for working capital. If the interest rates were higher, it would increase the cost of borrowings, and hence, increase the

repayment costs for debt. . The higher the level of debt-to-equity ratio for a company, the higher the decline in cash flow would be due to the impact of a rising interest rate.

<u>Lower revenues due to decreased consumer spending:</u> Most people these days have debts, whether it is an equated monthly installment (EMI) for a car or appliance, a mortgage, or credit card debts. Higher interest rates will translate into higher interest charges and, in turn, it is likely that the consumers would cut spending. This would particularly impact businesses that sell luxury items, which are sensitive to changes in income.

Currency fluctuations

Companies with overseas branches, or companies that trade internationally, are highly impacted by global currency fluctuations. Changes in currency exchange rates can significantly increase or decrease profits.

For instance, if a US-based company has a branch in Italy and makes EUR 1 million there, they would have ended up with $1.44 million in June 2011, but it would have reduced significantly by $200,000 in June 2012. These issues are very important when getting into contracts with international customers. Due to currency fluctuations, something may seem to be a good deal when it is contracted, but it could turn out to be not so profitable by the time it is fulfilled.

Companies can use a few strategies to counteract their currency exposure. One strategy is to lock into an exchange rate for a fixed period of time by getting into a **forward currency contract**. If you have estimated the interest rates to fall, this can be beneficial. If you need to pay your suppliers in another currency and you expect currency volatility in the future, you could buy foreign currency in advance.

Another strategy is to hedge against the currency exposure by using derivatives. Although this option is difficult to implement and complicated to understand, it could be highly effective in limiting exposure to volatility.

In conclusion, your company's external environment impacts the cash flow significantly. Industry and the economic environment impact all cash flows. For instance, if your company is in auto part manufacturing and that industry experiences a pronounced downturn, your revenues are likely to decrease or your expenses to make the sales would increase as it would require more effort to drive sales. Both would lead to a decrease in the operational cash flows. Changes in consumer's disposable income, interest rates, and currency fluctuations all impact the cash flow; hence, the company needs to adjust their strategies to cope with the changes.

KEY BUSINESS QUESTIONS

Current state

The answers to the following questions would allow you to analyze the current state of control over cash flows in your company and might offer precious insights about ways to boost your cash flow.

- What is the level of competition in the industry you operate in? Are you able to differentiate your offerings to gain a competitive advantage?
- Is your business impacted by high bargaining power of buyers or suppliers? Do you have strategies in place to counter the effect on your cash flow?
- Do you analyze cash flows and take remedial actions if needed?
- Is the operating cash your primary source of cash inflows?
- Does your company have optimum levels of leverage?

Six months from now

The answers to these questions would help you to gauge your progress in the past six months and would point out the most effective strategies.

- Were you able to overcome the challenges caused by the external environment?
- Do you use scenario analysis in your forecasting to analyze the impact of worst-case economic scenarios?
- How much has the cash flow improved in the past six months? What strategies have contributed most to the improvement?

Twelve months from now

The answers to these questions would help you to gauge your progress in the past 12 months.
- ✓ Were you able to overcome the challenges caused by the external environment?
- ✓ Did you notice any benefits of using scenario analysis in your forecasting to analyze the impact of worst-case economic scenarios?
- ✓ How much has the cash flow improved in the past twelve months? What strategies have contributed most to the improvement?

Cash Flow: A Quantitative Analysis

In this book, we will learn about managing cash flow for your company. However, before doing that, it is essential to understand the current situation and know all the metrics that could give you a clear picture in the future. The cash flow statement reveals how a business uses its cash (outflows) and where it gets its cash (inflows). It would have been so simple if we could think of net income as the easy way to evaluate a business's overall performance. However, that is not the case, as even though accrual accounting gives us a foundation to match sales income and expenses, it does not give us the value of the actual cash the business has generated from its profits. In this business environment where credit sales and purchase are predominant, this difference is likely to be crucial. In this chapter, we'll talk about what the financial statements and cash flow statement can reveal to you and where to find the information to evaluate critical evaluation metrics.

After reading this chapter, you will be able to:

- ✓ Understand the components of the cash flow statement
- ✓ Understand the metrics which could be used to gauge cash flow strength of the company
- ✓ Calculate and analyze the company's cash position using these metrics

Difference between profits and cash

At the very least, cash in a business or its liquidity is as important as its profitability. This is because a company's cash flow or cash position defines whether or not the company is making enough money to cover its obligations. In general, if a company is unprofitable for a couple of years, it could still go on, but if it cannot pay its bills it is more likely to go bankrupt. Despite this obvious fact, many business owners do not understand the importance of cash and only look at their company's income statement and ignore the cash flow statement.

> *Liquidity is at least as important as profitability if not more*

The cash flow statement gives us a visual representation of the amount of cash that comes in and goes out of the business over the specific reporting period. Although it sounds like the profit and loss statement, there is a considerable difference between the two. The main distinguishing factor is that profit and loss records work on accrual accounting (i.e., to record revenues and expenses when transactions occur), instead of when the actual cash is exchanged. Furthermore, the income statement also includes non-cash items, which are excluded from the cash flow statement.

Understanding your company's cash generating capacity and cash position is paramount in understanding a company's fundamentals. It gives us an idea about how or if the company would be able to pay for its day-to-day activities and future growth.

The cash flow statement

The **cash flow statement** has three distinct sections. Each of the sections is related to a particular business division, namely: operations, investing, and financing. In this book, we will discuss the management of all three activities in relation to cash flow. First, let's understand what is included in these three sections and what types of cash flow come under the respective headings.

Cash flow from investing

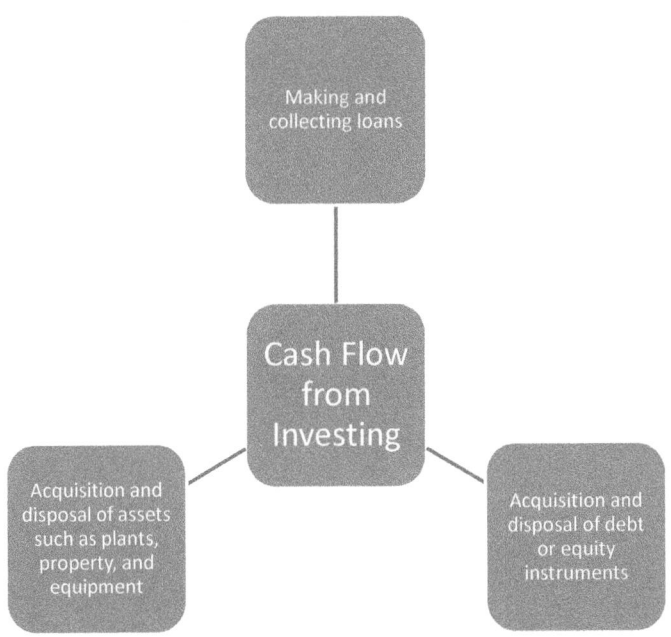

Most of the time, investment activities only create cash outflows, for instance capital expenditures for plants, property, and equipment, and purchasing securities for investment. Cash inflows are generated when these assets or investment securities are sold. Investment in securities is an integral part of managing excess cash, but a business owner needs to give special emphasis to the capital expenditure in this section as capital expenditures lead to a company's growth or the efficient running of its operations in order to remain competitive in the market.

Cash flow from financing

This category primarily consists of debt and equity transactions. Issuance of stock is much less common than borrowing as most companies engage in borrowing money on a regular basis.

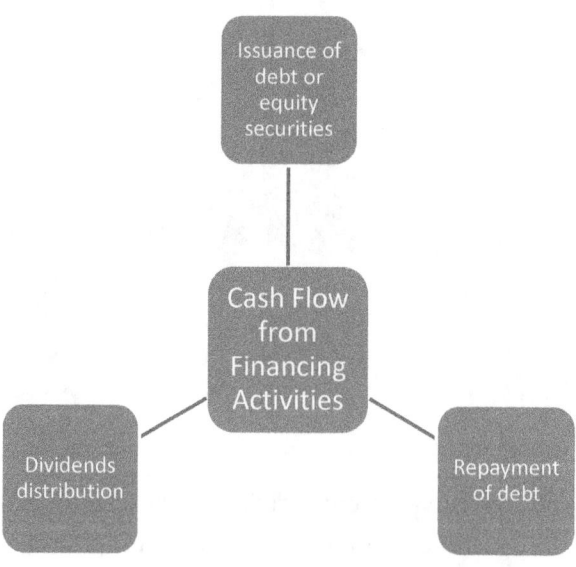

Cash flow from operations

This section includes the key cash inflows and outflows that are related to the everyday operations of the company:

Cash Inflows	Cash Outflows
• Cash sales • Accounts receivable collections	• Accounts payable • Payroll costs • Payroll taxes • Manufacturing/service expenses • Marketing/administrative expenses • Rents, income taxes • Insurance premiums

A simplified approach to cash flow analysis

Any business's cash flow can be identified as the figure that is calculated in the cash flow statement as net cash from operating activities. However, to actually gauge the business's health, value, and cash flow strength, there are three simple parameters that can be used. These are:

- EBITDA
- Free cash flow, and
- Operating cash flow

EBITDA means earnings before interest, taxes, depreciation, and amortization. It is a simple measure, which could be quickly calculated or at times given in the profit and loss statement of the company. EBITDA is calculated as:

> **EBITDA** = Operating Income + Depreciation + Amortization
> = EBIT + Depreciation + Amortization
> = Net Income + Income Tax Expense + Interest Expense + Depreciation + Amortization

In recent years, it has been extensively used to estimate the value of a business which is usually expressed as an EBITDA multiple. It has become a popular measure as it can be easily calculated, explained, and the information required calculating it is easily available from the main financial statements. However, as a measure of cash flow and operational strength of a company, it could have both strengths and weaknesses.

Some of these factors are:

Strengths	Weaknesses
• It indicates the operational strength. • Taxes could be treated as "non-operational" as they can be affected by accounting and, hence, do not impact the operational strength of the firm. • Interest is impacted by leverage, and not operations. • Depreciation again is impacted by the accounting methods used and, hence, cannot be used to gauge operational strength. • Amortization expense deals with the amortization of intangibles. Because it is an accounting convention, we know that it could also be impacted by accounting policies.	• EBITDA is not actual cash flow • It does not measure the actual cash available to service debt • It does not include changes in long-term debt • It does not include the impact on working capital • It does not include the impact of needed capital expenditures

Although EBITDA does not reflect in its entirety a company's available cash, or its ability to service debt, sustain its operations and growth potential, it is still a good measure, which could quickly give you an overview. However, EBITDA coupled with one or more measures can give you a much clearer picture.

Free cash flow

To overcome the deficiencies in EBITDA, we can calculate the company's **free cash flow (FCF)** metrics.

> **Free cash flow to firm (FCFF)** = EBIT (1-Tax) + non-cash charges (depreciation & amortization) - Change in non-cash working capital - CAPEX

Free cash flow to firm (FCFF) is a comprehensive free cash flow ratio. The FCFF represents the cash available after all important and essential cash outflows have been taken out (including taxes). The reason FCFF could be a better evaluation of a company's cash position is the **CAPEX** adjustment. Most companies spend cash to buy/repair/upgrade/replace their fixed assets. CAPEX can, therefore, cause a significant reduction in cash. If a business's cash generation capacity passes the FCFF test, it is likely to be in a position to avoid excessive borrowing, grow the business, pay dividends, and to survive crucial times.

Cash flow from operations (CFO)

CFO is generally calculated as:

> **CFO** = Net Income + Depreciation + Amortization - Changes in non-cash current assets (inventory, accounts receivables) + Changes in non-debt current liabilities (accounts payables, deferred revenue) + non-cash items
>
> = Net Income + Depreciation + Amortization – Changes in Non-Cash Working Capital + Non-Cash Charges

The key difference between EBITDA and CFO is that CFO also considers taxes and interest expense. Both generally exclude the non-cash and one-time or extraordinary expenses.

By calculating both EBITDA and FCF figures, a business owner is likely to get a clear understanding of the ability of the company to generate cash. After understanding this ability, he/she could compare this ability with the actual needs of the company and its future plans and goals.

In conclusion, once a business owner understands the importance of cash flow and how it is generated and reported, he/she could use these simple indicators to conduct a high-level analysis of the current situation of the firm. This approach will allow you to understand how the business is managing to pay its obligations and how it would make money in future.

KEY BUSINESS QUESTIONS

Current state

Cash flow analysis could address numerous questions regarding a firm's cash flow capabilities:
- ✓ Strength of the company's internal cash flow generation?
    - Is the cash flow from operations positive or negative?
    - What is the reason for it being negative, if it is?
    - Is it growth?
    - Is it lack of profitability?
    - Or is it mismanagement of working capital?
- ✓ Does the company have enough cash to meet its short-term obligations, such as interest and taxes, from its operating cash flow?
    - Can it continue to meet these obligations without reducing its operating flexibility?
- ✓ What is the company's investment in growth?

- Are these investments consistent with its business strategy?
- Did the company use internal cash flow to finance growth, or did it rely on external financing?

✓ Was the firm able to pay dividends from FCF, or did it have to resort to external financing?
- If the firm had to resort to external financing for paying its dividends, then is some analysis needed to determine if the company's dividend policy is sustainable?

✓ What type of external financing does the company rely on?
- Equity or debt?
- Is the financing option consistent with the company's overall risk appetite?

✓ Does the firm have any excess cash flow left after making capital investments?
- Is it a long-term trend?
- What plans does management have to deploy the free cash flow?

Financial Drivers of Cash Flow

Any company's cash flow is driven by a number of factors and it is important for every business owner to understand what these drivers are and how they impact a business's cash flow. In this chapter, we will understand the seven cash flow drivers and how they impact the cash flow. We will discuss each of these drivers in the subsequent chapters.

After reading this chapter, you will be able to:

- ✓ Understand the advantages of cash flow analysis and control
- ✓ Understand the components of a cash flow statement

Cash flow drivers

As cash flow is critically important for any business, understanding what primarily drives your company's cash flow is an excellent start in understanding how to manage cash flow. There are seven primary financial drivers for cash flow. Each of these drivers provide crucial information that, when brought together, is likely to help a business owner identify areas to focus on to improve cash flow and make better strategic business decisions. Understanding how to make use of this information to enhance your business's cash flow and operations is likely to improve your cash flow as well as your company's bottom line.

Main drivers of cash flow are:

Let us examine each of these.

Accounts receivable

Accounts receivables are one of the most significant drivers of cash flow. As most sales are on credit these days, the outstanding receivables at times could solve a company's cash crunch. In an ideal world, it would be optimum to make all the sales in cash; the second best option is to receive the cash payments for the sales before you pay for raw materials. Unfortunately, these are not common scenarios for most businesses.

> Accounts receivables constitute the most significant cash inflow

Hence, for most companies, the goal is to receive payment as soon as possible after making a sale, thereby reducing the number of accounts receivable days. Accounts receivable days are the number of days on average that it takes a customer to pay. Often, these are significantly different than the terms offered. The terms of repayment may be for instance, 30 days, such that a customer has 30 days to pay their invoice in full. However, often customers don't pay on time. So even though the terms for repayment are 15 or 30 days, the actual accounts receivable days could be much longer. The difference between an invoice date and a payment date can significantly impact a business's cash flow. The key here is to make the right sale to the right customer at the right time and in the right quantity and condition to encourage the customer's prompt payment.

Accounts payable

A business does not exist in isolation. It relies on suppliers and trading partners for raw materials or goods and services, which are essential for them to serve their customers. Accounts payable is one of the biggest contributors for cash outflows in a company. Most businesses have long-term purchase agreements with predetermined suppliers and they typically buy on credit; cash is paid to settle the debt when the payment becomes due. Hence, the faster a business transforms raw materials into products, the faster a company would be able to make its sales and collect cash.

The key to managing this driver is to increase the accounts payable days as much as possible without affecting your credibility as a buyer. Accounts payable days are the number of days a company takes on average to pay its suppliers. In general, accounts payable days are lower than the accounts receivable days for a company. This translates into suppliers being paid faster than cash collections from customers. This happens for small businesses primarily because most people do not like chasing money, but are easily convinced into paying before terms allow. Now, as the cash is going out to suppliers faster than its inflow from customers, it could result in a cash squeeze.

Accounts payables constitute the most significant cash outflow

Revenue growth

Most business owners when faced with a low cash flow scenario feel that selling more would fix their cash flow problem. However, what they need to understand is that, at times, selling more can actually make these problems worse.

This is because when you make a sale, you also generate expenses such as labor and raw materials, which most of the time are paid for before your customer has paid you. If you had an initial cash flow problem then sales growth could make it worse if you don't focus on other drivers. Hence, a business owner needs to understand that cash is generated from good customers. A good customer would be a customer who has a genuine need for your company's product or service and allows you to generate a healthy rate of return on investment.

Therefore, when focusing on sales growth with the aim of boosting cash flow, it is important to sell to the "right" customers as revenues from good customers is much more likely to result in increased cash flow faster.

Gross margin

Gross margin is basically net revenue less cost of goods sold. The higher the gross margin, the more gross income a company will have to cater to overheads and contribute in net profits. Gross margin is directly impacted by the **cost of goods sold (COGS)**, as even a small reduction in COGS would contribute directly to your profits. Hence, it is important to focus on reducing COGS.

Gross margin is the first step in getting to the company's profitability. Therefore, we should start the analysis from this step to reduce costs and increase profits. Profitability is the biggest contributor to your cash flow.

Profits generally translate into additional cash required for a number of actions.

Selling, general and administrative expense (SG&A)

In many companies, this could be termed differently but the most commonly used term for corporate overheads is **selling, general and administrative (SG&A)** expense. Reducing the SG&A directly impacts the company's net profits or the bottom line. A number of operational activities and costs come under this category. Many of these activities and their costs are necessary evils; there are some, which could be avoided/reduced and a focused analysis to figure out ways to reduce these costs, could significantly impact your net cash flow. To achieve a competitive advantage and enhance cash flow, an improvement drive for the internal processes might also be required. Specific goal setting or process improvement initiative could help the business in this respect.

Capital expenditure

Capital expenditures, popularly termed **CapEx**, are one of the best examples to demonstrate the divergence between cash flow and accounting income. For instance, if you purchase equipment for $500,000, you may decide to outlay the $500,000 in cash to make the purchase. However, the cost of the equipment will appear on the profit and loss statement as depreciation over the useful life of the equipment. The first month's report would show a few thousand in depreciation expense, but $500,000 disappeared from the cash pool.

CapEx is also significant as most investment costs are high. For instance, buying a fleet of cars for a cab company, investing in firm-wide software upgrades, or buying new warehouses are examples of capital expenditures that require significant amounts of cash. It is very important to analyze and understand if we are making the right decision. Why should we invest in a fleet of cars when we could lease them as well? Why invest in warehouses when so many companies are working "Just in Time." Capital expenditures should be avoided if there is no significant need or if the return on investment is too low as that cash could be used in revenue-generating activities.

Inventory

Inventory can be considered a necessary evil for a business. This is because to ensure timely delivery of orders, it is often necessary to maintain a level of inventory; however, inventory which is sitting idle in the warehouse consumes cash, and if cash is needed urgently, it can be difficult to liquidate. Hence, to store and move/transport surplus inventory drains cash from the working capital.

Risk costs like obsolescence and shrinkage; service costs like taxes, material handling, and interest all drain cash from the business. Furthermore, there is an opportunity cost as well, as the money that is tied up in inventory and the space used to store that inventory could be used for other more productive purposes. Hence, we understand that it is advisable to carry just the right amount of inventory so that you can manage customer orders, but avoid unnecessary costs. Reducing inventory days could do this. Inventory days are the average number of days stock sits in the warehouse waiting to be sold, while work in progress days is the average number of days jobs are in progress before invoicing. Both of these can be minimized by efficient sales forecasts. Reducing work in progress days would also have a positive impact on cash. This could be done by using checklists and templates to ensure consistent quality to reduce mistakes, and ultimately, wasted time.

> *Maintaining optimum inventory levels should be another focus point for managing cash flow of a business*

In conclusion, to be competitive in today's dynamic business environment, a business owner needs to manage cash very well. Supply chain and operational activities affect the seven primary cash drivers of a business in profound ways. Accounts payable, accounts receivable, revenue growth, gross margin, SG&A, and CapEx can all be more effectively managed with a strategic focus on operations.

All of these cash drivers act independently, but together, they constitute the business's cash-to-cash cycle. Understanding the link between operations and cash flow gives the business owner a base from where he/she can add on to the company's ability to sustain and grow. In the later chapters, we will learn to manage each one of these in detail.

Managing Cash: Inflows

Profits on paper look really good for your company, but a business needs cash to keep it going. Even more so for a small company, which may not have access to lines of credit to ease the short-term cash crisis – cash flow is king. For most companies, the key to cash flow management is in maximizing cash inflows and minimizing outflows. In this chapter, we will discuss the importance of managing operating cash inflows and the strategies for same.

After reading this chapter, you will be able to:

- ✓ Understand the impact of accounts receivables on cash flow
- ✓ Understand the importance of a shorter collection period
- ✓ Be able to use your accounts receivables' aging report to accelerate cash inflows
- ✓ Implement a cash flow friendly credit policy
- ✓ Understand the importance of factoring

Accounts receivables

Accounts receivables are one component, which significantly impacts cash flow. It represents the company's sales where the products or services have been delivered, but the cash has not yet been collected. In today's competitive environment, it becomes a necessity for most businesses to sell on credit; hence, payments of accounts receivables become a primary source of

Accelerate AR collection to boost cash

operating cash. Thus, a delayed payment from the customer's end could make it difficult for the business to meet its current obligations.

Collection period

The collection period is the time between the occurrence of the sale and the cash. If the collection period for a company is long, this means that the company has high investment in accounts receivable. Therefore, a shorter collection period is advisable. Financial gurus have even advised considering the pros and cons of eliminating the accounts receivable entirely (although this seems virtually impossible for practical purposes) by selling only for cash payments. The pros and cons of offering price discounts for partial upfront payments are also worth investigating.

Now to keep the collection period low, you need to know what it is and how it is calculated. Here is the most commonly used formula to calculate the average collection period:

Average Collection Period	$\dfrac{\text{Accounts receivables} \times \text{Number of days in the period}}{\text{Sales on credit}}$

For example, for the Judy's Products Ltd. company (see the case study listed in Appendix A, Tables 5 and 7), we would calculate the average collection period for Year 1 as follows:

> Sales on credit = $300,000 x 90% = $270,000
>
> Number of days in the period = 365
>
> Accounts receivable = $45,000
>
> **Average collection period** = 60.8 days

Now, if a company's average collection period is 60 days, then each sales dollar earned stays invested in accounts receivable for approximately 60 days. If this 60-day period covers the company's cash flow needs (i.e., if the company is able to run its day-to-day operations without feeling a cash crunch), then it is not mandatory to try to reduce the collection period. However, it would still help to reduce it as for those 60 days, the company could use that amount to invest and earn interest.

Hence, it is vital for businesses to seek and pursue opportunities to maximize cash inflows, and reduce collection periods. A company can figure out how much it needs to improve its collection period by looking at the industry averages.

Accounts receivable aging report

Now we know that we need to boost the cash inflows, but how exactly is this done? For this purpose, the accounts receivable aging report is a critical tool that can help in maintaining a company's financial health. This report primarily classifies accounts receivables based on the number of days the invoices have been past due.

The most important item to note in this report would be the customers' collection period that has extended beyond a 30 days term. Which is usually a term of 30 days. These customers need to be persistently contacted and, if needed, decisions must be made to change the sales strategy for them in the future (only cash on delivery, etc.). A thorough analysis of this report could lead the business owners to find early warning indicators of possible cash flow problems in the future.

Let us consider the sample-aging schedule displayed in Table 1 for Judy's Products Ltd. According to this aging schedule, it seems that the company needs to follow-up on collections with numerous customers, as there are many past the 30-day mark. However, the company needs to be even more aggressive with ZZZ Company, as there are a large number of orders that are past the 60-day mark and this customer seems to be holding payments for too long, perhaps to enhance their own cash flow situation.

Table 1: Accounts receivables aging schedule for Judy's Products Ltd

Customer Name	Total Accounts Receivables	1–30 Days Past Due	31–60 Days Past Due	Over 60 Days Past Due
ABC Company	10,000	5,000	10,000	
XYZ Company	5,000	5,000	----	----
LMNO Company	4,500	4,000	----	500
PQRS Company	11,500	6,000	4,000	1,500
ZZZ Company	6,600	1,000	1,600	4,000
RST Company	7,400	7,400	----	----
Total	45,000	28,400	15,600	6,000

As a general rule, a company should set a comfortable collection period as their target, say 30 days. After that, the company needs to find the customers whose invoices have passed the 30-day mark and contact them on a regular basis. However, if despite your best efforts the customer still delays payment or does not pay, then some tough decisions need to be made in terms of future sales to that customer. Strategies that could be used are future sales only on cash on delivery terms and holding deliveries until previous invoices are cleared; also, in some cases, it might be necessary to stop future sales.

Send the invoice out as soon as possible!

The aging schedule also shows us some early indicators of future trouble, such as recent changes in payment schedule by some customers. It also helps a company to avoid wasting their time and energy chasing customers who regularly pay within the comfortable limit.

In the example we discussed above, Judy's Products needs to use their time and effort chasing ZZZ Company, because if ignored, this could turn into a bad debt, thus negatively impacting the cash balances.

Collection process and system

Ideally, it would be optimum for businesses to collect cash at the time of sale or delivery or in advance from customers. However, it is very difficult in today's business scenario; hence, it is vital to have an efficient cash management process in order to keep the accounts receivables at a manageable level.

A number of factors help in running effective cash management process:

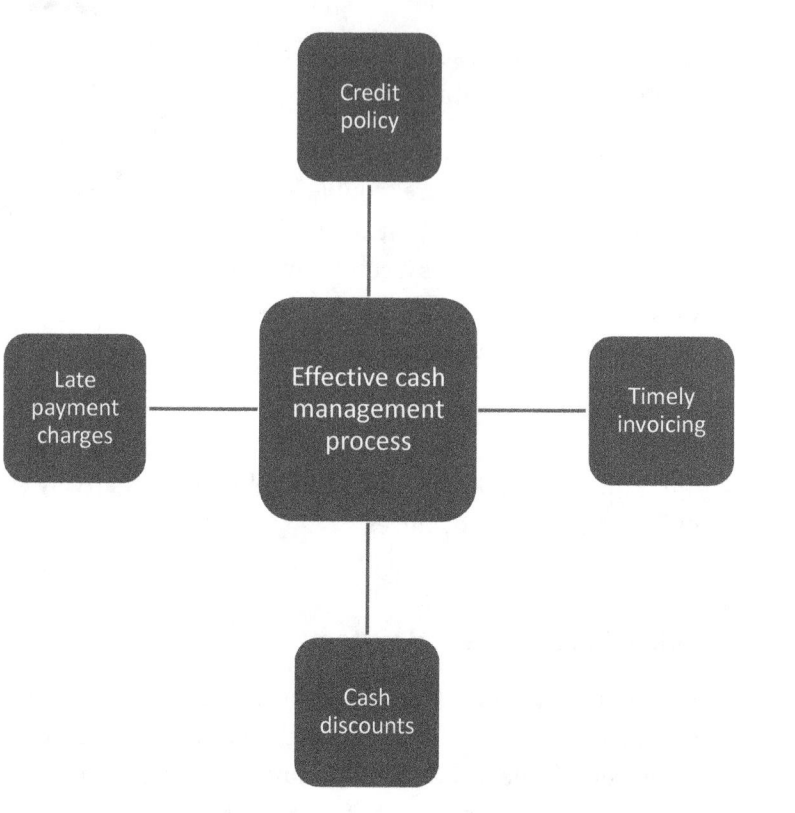

Credit Policy

It is important to have a credit policy and strictly adhere to it. The credit policy should include a time limit for cash collection (say 30 days), a time limit within which the company is comfortable managing its cash flow. The credit policy also needs to include a credit limit (say $5,000) beyond which credit should not be

Creating and enforcing a credit policy could help avoid cash flow problems

extended to a customer. If a customer reaches the credit limit, then further sales should be either cash on delivery or an extension of credit limit could be considered based on the past payment schedule and relationship with the customer. Ideally, the credit policy could define the collection period, but it is practically a rarity as some customers are likely to pay early while others might be late. However, it gives a benchmark to analyze customers as well as the business's cash flow requirements.

It is a good idea to indulge in a thorough credit check for the customer before doing business with them. This proves to be highly beneficial in reducing or avoiding bad debts at a later date.

Timely invoicing

One of the most important things that a company can do for accelerating its cash inflows is to enhance their internal systems in such a way that an invoice could be generated and sent to the customer at the earliest. This is the most important practice for good cash flow management as the complete cash collection process starts after the customer has received the invoice.

Another critical point is that invoices should be accurate as even a small mistake can delay the payment process. If you are a small company and your customers are other smaller companies, then they would also try to delay the payments as much as possible to boost their cash flow. An inaccurate invoice could, therefore, give them all the more reason to delay the payments.

Business owners should analyze current present invoicing practices, and take steps to cater to the inefficiencies, if there are any.

Cash discounts

A thorough analysis is needed in this respect if offering cash discounts for early payments is essential to compete in the marketplace and remain viable. If not essential, it might help to maintain or increase a business's market share. A careful analysis is needed as the cash discount would help to reduce the investments in accounts receivables and positively impact cash flow, but it might negatively impact the expected revenue. If it is necessary, then a policy should be established regarding the percentage of discount on offer and the time period.

Late payment charges

As cash discounts are an incentive to pay early, late payment charges penalize customers who do not honor the offered credit terms. However, for a small business, collecting finance charges could prove to be difficult or could even harm the business if the customer decides to take their business elsewhere. If a company has a late payment charge policy or wants to add it, to avoid the potential pitfalls, a thorough cost benefit analysis should first be made before implementing the policy.

Up to now, we have discussed only internal systems that could help a company in enhancing their cash inflows. There are some external methods as well which could be used to boost cash flows in times of need. There are times when despite your best efforts you could land in a cash flow crisis. These methods are useful under such circumstances. One of the most important ones, which we will discuss here, is factoring.

Factoring

Factoring is primarily a way to boost your short-term cash flow if need be. It can also be called accounts receivable financing. The company sells its accounts receivables or invoices to a third party called the **factor**.

Here's how factoring works:

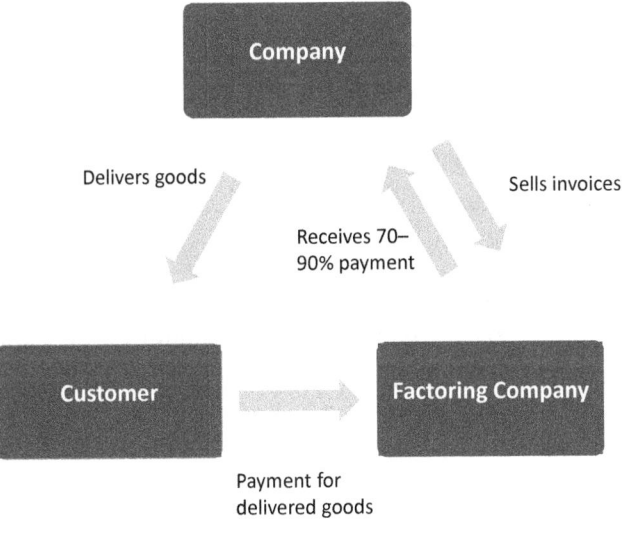

A company sells its account receivables to the factoring company. The factoring company usually advances 70–90% of the total invoice amount. They then notify the customers and receive the payments from them. Once they receive the money, they usually pay the balance of the sum after subtracting their fee.

Factoring could be a good option to boost short-term cash flow without acquiring any debt. However, if you decide to use this route, do your research and hire a company most suited for your needs. Carefully discuss the terms and how they will be communicated to your customers. You need to ensure that they treat your customers right as a customer's bad experience with the factoring company could potentially impact your future sales.

In conclusion, a company needs to devote ample time for its accounts receivable. Ideally, the accounts receivable collection process should start before doing business with a client by having a thorough credit check. Later, a number of strategies as mentioned above could be used to keep your receivables streamlined, which is vital for cash flow management.

In times of need, factoring is also a good option to boost short-term cash flow. It is also a very good option to manage cash flow for companies working in industries that have a very long cash conversion cycle.

In this chapter, we have learned practical methods to boost your cash flow by managing and accelerating the cash inflows. In the next chapter, we will discuss how to boost your cash flow by managing cash outflows.

KEY BUSINESS QUESTIONS

Current state

The answers to the following questions will allow you to analyze the current state of your operating cash inflows and might offer precious insights about ways to boost your cash flow.
- ✓ What is your investment in accounts receivables currently? Is it at an acceptable level? Is it less than or equal to the industry average?
- ✓ What is your collection period? Is it less than or equal to the industry average?
- ✓ Does your current collection period allow you to meet your obligations?
- ✓ Does your company create an accounts receivable aging schedule on a regular basis? Are you aware which of your customers are the worst offenders in terms of late payments?
- ✓ Do you regularly follow-up with those customers whose invoices have passed the due date of the credit terms?
- ✓ Do you have a set credit policy? Do you strictly adhere to it?

Six months from now

The answers to these questions will help you to gauge your progress in the past six months and will point out the most effective strategies.
- ✓ What is your investment in accounts receivables? Is it less than or equal to the industry average?
- ✓ What is your collection period? Is it less than or equal to the industry average? How much has it improved in the past six months? What strategies have contributed most to the improvement?
- ✓ Does your current collection period allow you to meet

- your obligations?
- ✓ What benefits did you notice by creating an accounts receivable aging schedule on a regular basis? Are you aware which of your customers are the worst offenders in terms of late payments?
- ✓ Do you regularly follow-up with the customers whose invoices have passed the due date of the credit terms?
- ✓ Have you created a credit policy? Do you strictly adhere to it?

Twelve months from now

The answers to these questions will help you to gauge your progress in the past 12 months.
- ✓ Is your investment in accounts receivables at an acceptable level now?
- ✓ Does your current collection period allow you to meet your obligations?
- ✓ How much has your collection improved in the past six months? What strategies have contributed most to the improvement?
- ✓ Do you have a set process now for creating an accounts receivables aging schedule regularly?
- ✓ Do you regularly follow-up with the customers whose invoices have passed the due date of the credit terms?
- ✓ What are the challenges you are facing in adhering to the credit policy?
- ✓ Is your credit policy now on par with industry standards? What is the credit term used by your competition?

Managing Cash: Outflows

In the last chapter, we discussed strategies for maximizing cash inflows. In this chapter we will discuss the other most important aspect of managing operating cash flow, which is minimizing (or delaying as much as possible) cash outflows.

After reading this chapter, you will be able to:

- ✓ Understand the impact of accounts payables on cash flow
- ✓ Understand the importance of a longer creditor period
- ✓ Be able to use your accounts payables aging report
- ✓ Implement a cash flow friendly payment policy
- ✓ Understand the importance of managing a "cash pool"

Main cash outflows for a business

The main operational areas where large amounts of cash flows out from the business are: accounts payables, payrolls, taxes, and other operating expenses. In this chapter, we will discuss these three one by one.

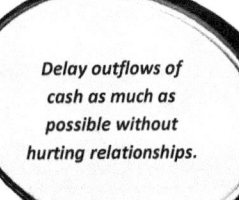
Delay outflows of cash as much as possible without hurting relationships.

Accounts payables

This is the most important component of operational outflows that significantly impacts cash flow. It represents the company's purchases where the products or services have been received but the cash has not yet been paid.

Creditor days

Creditor days or **days payable outstanding (DPO)** is the time between receiving the product or service and the actual outflow of cash for it. This number tells us how a company is doing with suppliers. Strictly speaking from a cash flow perspective, a longer DPO is advisable. Practically speaking, this means that effectively your suppliers are lending you money to buy from them; thus, you can use this cash somewhere else in the business, where it might be more immediately needed. If the DPO period for a company is short as compared to the industry average, then it could mean that the company is not taking advantage of the payment terms offered by its suppliers. However, careful analysis is needed for upfront payments for certain discounts. If your company is not facing a potential or ongoing cash flow problem, then taking advantage of cash discounts could be beneficial.

Now, in order to keep the DPO period high, you need to know how it is calculated. Here is the most commonly used formula to calculate the average creditor days:

Average days payables outstanding	$\dfrac{\text{Account payables} \times \text{Number of days in the period}}{\text{Cost of sales}}$

Where Cost of Sales = Cost of goods sold + Ending inventory − Starting inventory

Let us understand the impact of DPO with the help of an example. Let us consider the case of Judy's Products Ltd. (see the case study listed in Appendix A, Tables 5 and 7); we would calculate the DPO period for Year 1 as follows:

> Cost of Sales = $ 60,000 - 19248 + 23,049
>
> = $63,801
>
> Number of Days in the period = 365
>
> Accounts payable = $4,503
>
> **Average days payable outstanding =**
>
> 25.76 days

Now, if a company's average collection period is 60 days and average DPO is 25.76 days it could be a huge problem for future cash flows due to the huge gap in the timing of cash inflows and outflows. However, if the company is able to run its day-to-day operations without feeling a cash crunch, then it is not mandatory to try to increase the DPO period and it could be more beneficial to take the discount for early payment if the supplier is offering any. If there is no discount offered, then it is worth considering increasing the DPO period, as the cash in your bank account would be earning interest for a few more days, however meager.

After all is said, it is essential to understand that simply cutting down your collection period or increasing your DPO are not necessarily sound long-term solutions. Effective management of cash flow entails management of all the aspects of the cycle, including efficient business processes and enhanced credit management.

Accounts payable aging schedule

Similar to the accounts receivables aging schedule which shows the accounts receivables based on the number of days the invoices are past due, the accounts payable aging schedule shows the accounts payable based on the number of days the invoices are past due. It is a critical tool for a company in determining the efficiency of invoice payments. Although it is a good strategy to delay payment until the invoice is due from a cash flow management perspective. The company should be careful about relying too much on its trade credit. This could stretch your goodwill, which might impact future credit terms. The management should be even more careful to avoid late payments; along with impacting goodwill, it might impact the supplier's business (especially if it's a small company), which would ultimately negatively impact your own business.

An accounts payable aging report looks very similar to an accounts receivable aging schedule. The difference is just that instead of showing the cash your customers owe you, it shows the cash that you owe your suppliers. It is a good idea to create an accounts payable aging schedule fortnightly or at least at the end of each month.

Let us consider the sample aging schedule displayed below for Judy's Products Ltd. The number of columns in the table can be adjusted according to your requirements; for example, you could list the outstanding amounts in 15-day intervals instead of 30-day intervals. Looking at the aging schedule could help in spotting potential problems in payables management and, hence, help you protect your company from major trade credit troubles. According to this aging schedule, it seems that the company needs to pay CCC Company and then BBB Company in order to protect the established goodwill for the trade credit.

Table 2: Accounts payables aging schedule for Judy's Products Ltd

Supplier Name	Total Accounts Payable	Current	1-30 Days Past Due	31-60 Days Past Due	Over 60 Days Past Due
AAA Company	1,000	1,000	----		
BBB Company	500	300	200	----	----
CCC Company	1,500	1000	----	500	----
DDD Company	303	303	----	----	----
EEE Company	1,200	1,200	----	----	----
Total	4,503	3,803	200	500	0

The schedule is also an important tool for managing and improving a business's cash flow. In the above example it shows that Judy's Products Ltd needs at least $3,803 this month to pay off its payables for this month (as this is a monthly schedule; in the case of a fortnightly schedule, the total current amount would be due within a fortnight).

Payment process and system

Businesses need efficient processes to control their cash outflows. One of the most widely used, and a reliable method is centralization of the payments of accounts payables. This helps in scheduling companywide payments as well as paying as late as possible.

In terms of cash outflows, two of the most important factors that help in running an effective cash management process are **payment systems** and **payment policy**:

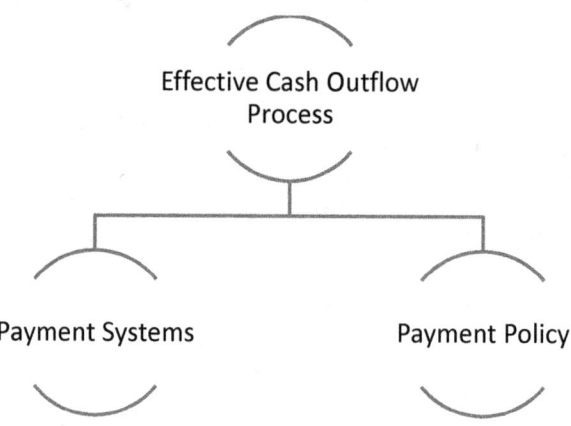

Payment systems

It is important to have a system in place for your payment processing that is streamlined and efficient. The following would be the most important aspects in having a payment system in place:

Do not pay early
In the earlier section of this chapter, we discussed the importance of paying your invoices as late as possible. Thus, while setting up your accounts payable process, it is important that you make use of the accounts payable aging schedule and pay the invoices just when they are due. Keep track of the amount of cash needed to pay the "current" invoices in a particular period and make sure you have the cash available to pay on time. If the terms from your vendor are net 30 days that means that the supplier expects to be paid in 30 days; hence, there is no need to pay earlier unless and until you can derive a special benefit by paying early (such as a discount).

Double check the invoices
This is immensely important as even a simple mistake in an invoice, such as the difference of a cent here or there in a unit price, could lead to a difference of thousands of dollars in the total amount. Once an incorrect invoice is paid, and you realize it later, you would have to go through the elaborate process of getting a refund. There should be a designated employee responsible for approving all incoming invoices.

An internal reviews of invoices, especially if the amount is large, cannot be stressed enough. Have regular internal cost audits to determine that **the goods or services purchased are really needed and explore less expensive alternatives.** The money saved by this activity would enhance a company's cash flows as well as profits.

Consider investing in a computerized system
Economically priced software installations could also help you with integrating and automating your planning, budgeting, purchasing, payables, and receivables. Though these inexpensive systems might have limited functionality (such as no reporting), they can be effective in helping you control over payment amounts, timings, and whether cash is available to pay them. This could help in avoiding unpleasant surprises.

Thus, we see that an effective accounts payable system ensures:

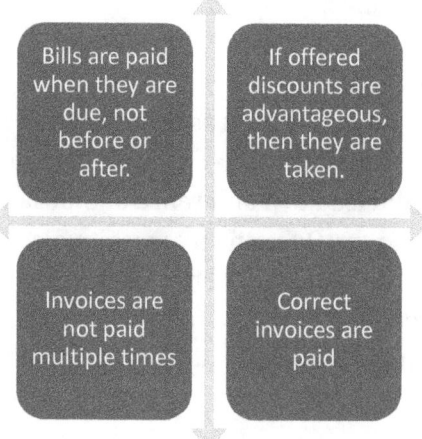

Payment policy

A payment policy should be created after considerable thought and analysis, as it is not only vital for your cash flow, but it is also is critical for building a good relationship with your suppliers.

Have clarity of your purchasing objectives
In general, a vendor is selected based on his product quality and reliability. Price and credit terms are also important factors. If in your industry the bargaining power of suppliers is not very high, then you can shop around and try to find a supplier with flexible credit terms while offering the same quality and reliability.

Agree on the payment terms in writing
Write a general payment policy and help the suppliers understand your payment terms. If your terms are different from their terms, then make sure that you have a written agreement before you order.

Have some flexibility
You should be prepared to trade off credit if there is some better benefit on offer, such as a discount for full or partial cash payment upfront.

Communicate with your suppliers
If you regularly pay on time, then it is likely that your suppliers would do you a favor by extending your credit term if you need it sometime. However, keep in mind to

communicate to them beforehand if you believe you will not be able to pay on time.

Managing your payroll, taxes, and other operating expenses

Payroll
For most companies, payroll is one of the largest cash outflows every month. To keep this outflow in check, the most popular trend is to have a flexible workforce. You could try outsourcing certain jobs or hiring temporary workers who can be hired on needs basis. It is essential to have full-time employees for core activities, otherwise business growth would suffer; but, for other non-essential activities, outsourcing could be a good option.

Taxes
Taxes again are one of the most important cash outflows. Though it cannot be avoided, it could be delayed by using strategies such as using accelerated depreciation for taxation.

Other operating expenses
Inventory: There are a number of hidden costs that are related to inventory which could impact cash flow, such as storage, spoilage, etc. It is a good idea to remove obsolete inventory immediately.
Insurance: Though it is important to insure your business, you need to be sure not to over insure. Purchasing group packages for insurance generally leads to the lowest premiums. Make sure you cover all the important risks but avoid duplication.

Managing a cash pool

A cash pool refers to a cash buffer, which companies should manage to cater to unforeseen circumstances. Even if your cash flow is smooth and you are currently not facing any issues, it is always prudent to manage a small cash pool so that you are not cash-strapped in the case of an unlikely event. A cash pool could be the difference between smooth operations and operations grinding to a stop if something unforeseen happen.

The size of the cash pool depends on the business. You could use data such as past cash flow history, future sales prospects, and other forecasts to analyze and arrive at an optimum cash pool level for your business. You also need to balance the cost of the cash pool (i.e., the opportunity cost of the money lying idle with the potential damage that could be caused by being cash-strapped at an opportune moment).

In conclusion, an effective cash management system would keep the cash outflows in check Paying the invoices only when they become due is the simplest and most effective way to manage cash outflow, but it is ignored in many small businesses. Despite making your best efforts in managing operational inflows and outflows, there are times when an unforeseen circumstance could negatively impact the cash flows and potentially damage the business. Hence, it is increasingly important in today's ever-changing business environment to manage a cash pool.

In this chapter, we have learned practical methods to boost your cash flow by managing and delaying the cash outflows. In the next chapter, we will discuss how to boost your cash flow by optimizing your sales function.

KEY BUSINESS QUESTIONS

Current state

The answers to the following questions will allow you to analyze the current state of your operating cash outflows and might offer precious insights about ways to boost your cash flow.

- ✓ What is your level of accounts payable currently? Is it similar to the industry average?
- ✓ What is your DPO period? Is it similar to the industry average?
- ✓ Is your current DPO period in line with the terms offered by your customers or are you consistently paying early?
- ✓ Does your company create an accounts payable aging schedule on a regular basis? Are you aware if you are late in payments to any of your suppliers?
- ✓ Do you inform the suppliers on time if you are unable to pay an invoice by its due date?
- ✓ Do you have a set payment policy? Do you adhere to it?
- ✓ Do you carefully manage your expenses such as insurance, payrolls? Do you have any non-essential personnel?
- ✓ Do you maintain a cash buffer to cater to unforeseen circumstances?

Six months from now

The answers to these questions will help you to gauge your progress in the past six months and will point out the most effective strategies.
- ✓ What is your level of accounts payable? Is it similar to the industry average?
- ✓ What is your DPO period? Is it less than or equal to the industry average? How much has it improved in the past six months? What strategies have contributed most to its improvement?
- ✓ What benefits did you notice by creating an accounts payables aging schedule on a regular basis? Are you aware of which payments are due to your suppliers in the next 30 days?
- ✓ Do you have a set payment policy? Do you adhere to it?
- ✓ Have you started building your cash pool?

Twelve months from now

The answers to these questions will help you to gauge your progress in the past 12 months.
- ✓ What is your level of accounts payable? Is your DPO period similar to the industry average now?
- ✓ What strategies have contributed most to the improvement of your DPO?
- ✓ Do you have a set process now for creating an accounts payables aging schedule regularly?
- ✓ What are the challenges you are facing in adhering to the payment policy?
- ✓ Is your payment policy now on par with industry standards? What are the payment terms used by your competition?
- ✓ Is your cash pool at an optimum level?

Optimizing Your Sales Function

Often, small business owners believe that cash flow management is primarily a financial function and we should leave that responsibility with the accountant. However, it is important to understand that cash inflow and outflow mainly occurs from operations, such as selling the product or service for inflowing cash and purchasing raw materials and paying salaries for outflowing cash.

Hence, it is important for operating staff to understand how the cash flows in the business. In today's competitive environment, it is essential that operating staff not only take care of client satisfaction and profit generation, but also to enhance the cash flow.

The sales function needs to carry out their tasks with cash flow awareness. They should know the impact of making a certain sale to a certain customer on the business's cash flow. In this chapter, we will discuss one of the most important parts of the business. Although not exactly cash focused, it has the highest impact on a business's cash flow.

After reading this chapter, you will be able to:

- ✓ Understand the true purpose of sales function
- ✓ Understand the objectives of sales function to maintain a sustainable business
- ✓ Be able to understand the importance of sales forecast
- ✓ Be able to do a basic product analysis

Purpose of the sales function

The purpose of existence of most businesses is to make money. However, any business's survival depends on providing quality products and services as well as diligent cash conversion. A customer's needs and the business's ability to fulfil those needs keep it in business. The sales team is essentially the link between the business and its clients, and customer service is mainly driven by the sales function. Hence, it is important for the sales team to sell ethically and to the right clients. Often, the sales team's sole emphasis is to enhance the top line as much as possible (probably motivated by result-based compensation plans), but this mindset needs to change for the long-term survival of a business.

The sales function needs to emphasize the following:

- ✓ Your top priority should be providing good quality goods and services to the customers that are suitable for their particular needs. The focus should be on the client's welfare as that would lead to high customer satisfaction and, hence, prosperity for both parties.
- ✓ While selling, keep in mind the profit margin for that particular sale.
- ✓ Take time to create a sales forecast and plan for the short- and long-term.
- ✓ Make sure the sale adds cash flow to the business with profits. Hence, it is important that the sales person assists with the smooth collection of debts. The sales person, in communications with clients, must always

resolve any issues quickly to avoid a time when the customer does not want to pay.
- ✓ Correlate actual customer sales directly with management's long- and short-term plans.
- ✓ Make sure that the sales team and compensation plans are in line with the company's long-term plan.
- ✓ Integrate the sales function with other functions as much as possible.

The sales function's objective is not just selling but providing efficient service to keep the customer happy. If the objective of the sales team were only to sell for a higher revenue number every quarter, it would lead to deteriorating client relationships. This will impact the future revenue profits as well as cash flows. An unhappy customer is highly unlikely to give you repeat business. It is even more difficult to extract timely payments from unhappy or dissatisfied customers.

Never compromise on quality

Ideally, the business's aim should be to provide the best quality product while maintaining good profits and cash flow. This would lead to growth of your business as well as the client's business. However, to achieve this, the sales staff should be aware of the company's strategic plans. They should know the company's strategic direction and streamline their sales efforts in line with the overall company strategy.

Objectives of sales function

As mentioned previously, the sales function of any company should be integrated with other functions so the whole business works in sync. Keeping that in mind, the sales function of any company should have four main objectives:

1. Strive for continuous improvement and deliver quality products
2. Reduce costs
3. Research product development
4. Manage change

Let us discuss all of these in detail.

1. Strive for continuous improvement and deliver quality products

The first and foremost objective is to strive for continuous improvement in terms of your product/service delivery and delivering quality products to the customers. Keep in touch with customers, ask for their feedback, and understand the customer's expectations. It is essential to exceed or at least meet the customer's expectations to achieve customer satisfaction, which would in turn lead to timely payments. A satisfied customer is also likely to give you repeat business and, hence, enhance future revenue and profits.

Meeting customer expectations → Satisfied customer → Revenue and profit improvement → Cash improvement

2. Reduce costs

An optimized sales function should also help in reducing costs. A sales team striving for customer satisfaction would be better acquainted with customer's requirements and satisfaction levels, which would lead to better sales forecasts. Improved and reliable forecasts would also help to reduce inventory-carrying costs, as only the required inventory would be carried. By reducing the time wasted on unnecessary meetings and follow-ups, labor costs would be reduced.

3. Research product development

The sales function should identify their target market correctly. As they are directly in touch with the customers (i.e., the target market), it is much easier for them to research the needs and wants of the market. They could gather valuable intel about any product enhancements that the market needs or if any new product or service is growing in demand, and the business could potentially benefit by introducing it. In today's competitive environment, the product life is decreasing. If a company could incorporate these valuable insights into their offerings and then work to bring them quickly to market, the business could gain first mover advantage. Also, a faster turnaround of the ideas into product offerings would lead to faster recovery of the investment in the introduction of a new product.

4. Manage change

We all know that change is the only constant in life. However, in this context, managing change would be adapting faster to the changing market environment, demands, and trends. If a company is able to continuously improve while adapting to the ever-changing market environment, it gains a competitive advantage. The main issues that a company could need to address are:

Sales planning drives organizational planning

Changes in buyer behavior: The current generation of professionals usually demand better product explanations and higher service levels in order to maintain their loyalty to one company. Thus, the sales function must be staffed with better-trained sales professionals who can offer professional customer service, in order to close orders and engage the customers for a longer term.

<u>Changes in the remuneration systems:</u> The external business environment these days is highly competitive, leading to very tight profit margins for most products or services. Thus, it might take more effort and higher competency to close orders. The impact of the changes in the external environment could also be that the remuneration plans for sales need to be reconsidered.

<u>Changes in technology:</u> With technological advancements, we have seen a great deal of changes in how we record and report sales. As businesses improve their productivity by using better technology, the sales professionals also need to educate themselves about those new technologies to perform effectively.

As we define the sales function objectives, it has become more and more apparent that all the business functions need to work together to develop a successful and sustainable business.

Sales planning and forecasting

To complete organizational planning, reliable sales forecasts are essential. These impact the inventory planning, purchase planning, payroll planning, and so on. Therefore, for most businesses, the first step in effective organizational planning is to work on reliable sales forecasts. Ideally, 80 percent of a sales forecast should consist of actual customer orders. This can be accomplished by effective communication with the customers.

The management in conjunction with the sales function should determine the products or services they should sell in the plan period. They need to analyze past trends, current and potential customer demand for the product or service, competitive factors, resource allocation, profit margins, etc. Here is an example of such a product analysis:

Table 3. Revenues and profits as per product segments for Judy's Products Ltd

Product	Price	Cost	Gross Profit	Unit Sales	Revenue	% Of Revenue	Gross Profit
AA	5	4	1	140	700	2.24%	140
BB	12	7	5	1,800	21,600	69.01%	9,000
CC	45	20	25	200	9,000	28.75%	5,000
				2,140	31,300	100.00%	14,140

Judy's Products Ltd. has three products: AA, BB, and CC. These are primarily three different types of soap products catering to different target markets. Now, based on the above table, the company wants to analyze and determine the future of these three products. Let's start with product AA; it is a low cost and low price product, which has low profit margins as compared to the company's other products. Furthermore, it seems that the demand for the product is less as the company is selling a handful of units of this product and is not even able to realize the economies of scale by bulk production and sale. This product is basically fulfilling the needs of a very small target market for the company, the consumers who are cost conscious. Now, due to the low level of return, the company might consider not tying up its resources, such as staff, equipment, and cash, with this product. While we do not see the cash contribution of this product in the table, it is likely to be small due to the low level of unit sales and low profit margin.

Product BB is the company's flagship product, bringing in about 70 percent of the revenue. Due to high unit sales and high profit margin, this product is likely to significantly contribute to the cash flow. The sales team needs to call the customers buying this product to get sales commitments while making the sales forecasts. Product CC is the top of the range product, and although the unit sales for this product are lower than AA, its profit margin is much higher. The company should plan individually for each of the products whether to increase, decrease, or simply maintain the sales levels. Once the strategy is decided, the efforts should be made in the correct direction. While making the decision, the cash flow impact of each of the products should be considered.

Sales function and cash flow

We understood that the sales function should be an integral part of the business's strategic plan. The sales function must consider every customer as well as each sale as a standalone profit and cash flow center. This means that each sale should lead to profit and should also positively contribute to the business's cash flow. Also, special consideration should be given to the sales team's remuneration policy. The targets for the salespeople should not be solely revenue-based, but should instead be based on cash flow, as the aim is not just to increase revenue, but cash flow as well.

It is also important to control the costs as not only would it increase profits, but it would also allow for charging the customers less and increasing sales volumes. Along with product costs, all operating costs such as processing collections, customer service, etc., must also be considered. We will discuss the cost considerations in much greater detail in the next two chapters.

In conclusion, the sales function should operate in the clear strategic direction set by top management in collaboration with the operating functions. The sales function should keep customer service and cash generation as its top priority. In a small business or in any business, it should not be acceptable to make sales that cannot be delivered or if the sale positively contributes to the salesperson's commission, but has a negative impact on the company's cash flow.

KEY BUSINESS QUESTIONS

Current state

The answers to the following questions will allow you to analyze the current state of your operating cash inflows and might offer precious insights about ways to boost your cash flow.

- ✓ Do you create a sales forecast and product analysis?
- ✓ Does your sales function monitor its performance with respect to the plan?
- ✓ Was your key sales staffing part of the planning process?
- ✓ Does your company culture allow the sales staff to freely take initiative?
- ✓ Does your key sales staff understand the strategic direction of the company?
- ✓ Does the method of compensation used for your sales staff support progress toward the company's goals?
- ✓ Do you perform product analysis so that the company's resources are more effectively utilized?
- ✓ Is the sales function motivated to be aware of the current market such as new developments in relation to competitors, clients, product innovation, etc.?

Six months from now

The answers to these questions would help you to gauge your progress in the past six months and would point out the most effective strategies.

- ✓ Did you create a process for making sales forecasts and performing product analysis?
- ✓ Do you plan to monitor the plan's performance with respect to the plan?
- ✓ Was your key sales staffing part of the planning process?
- ✓ Are your key sales staffs now in sync with the strategic direction of the company?
- ✓ What benefits did you notice by aligning the method of compensation used for your sales staff with your

company's goals?
- ✓ What benefits did you notice from performing product analysis?
- ✓ Is the sales function now more motivated to be aware of the current market, such as new developments in relation to competitors, clients, product innovation, etc.?
- ✓ How much has the cash flow improved in the past six months? What strategies have contributed most to the improvement?

Twelve months from now

The answers to these questions will help you to gauge your progress in the past 12 months.

- ✓ Did you create a process for making sales forecasts and performing product analysis?
- ✓ Do you plan to monitor the plan's performance with respect to the plan?
- ✓ What were the potential benefits of creating sales forecasts and then monitoring it?
- ✓ Did your key sales staff get a chance to contribute to the planning process?
- ✓ Are your key sales staffs now in sync with the strategic direction of the company?
- ✓ What benefits did you notice by aligning the method of compensation used for your sales staff with your company's goals?
- ✓ What benefits did you notice from performing product analysis?
- ✓ Is the sales function now more motivated to be aware of the current market, such as new developments in

- relation to competitors, clients, product innovation, etc.?
- ✓ How much has the cash flow improved in the past 12 months? What strategies have contributed most to the improvement?

Cost Optimization: Benchmarking

Measuring a company's progress is crucial for its successful management. If a business is unaware of its standing in any particular process, it cannot fathom if it is on target, behind target, or ahead of target. In the current business environment, it is simply not enough to only be doing as well as the next competitor. If a business is behind its competition, it is highly likely that they would lose long-term revenue and market share. To gain and then try to maintain the competitive advantage, businesses need to aim for continuous improvement and be the best in their field.

Furthermore, every business is under increasing pressure to control costs while providing enhanced value to its stakeholders. The most effective way to apply cost controls is to apply it against opportunities that have the potential to achieve the highest return for the effort.

Costs ↓
Cash Flow ↑

As discussed in the previous chapter, increased sales enhance the cash flow of the company. However, an increase in sales only contributes a sum equivalent to the profit margin of the cash flow. If we look at a decrease in cost, it contributes a dollar-for-dollar amount to the cash flow. Hence, we see that cost control contributes more to positive cash flow and the company has much more control over costs than revenue; hence, it is somewhat more easily achievable

In this chapter and the next, we will focus on two techniques to control costs in an organization:

- Benchmarking, and
- Activity-based costing

We will focus on benchmarking practices in this chapter. After reading this chapter, you will be able to:

- ✓ Understand what benchmarking is
- ✓ Understand the benchmarking process
- ✓ Use benchmarking to control costs

Although a reduction in costs would lead to an improvement in cash flow, cost controls should be balanced and well analyzed so that they do not negatively impact the normal functioning of the company. Thus, simply reducing costs by any means necessary should not be the focus of this exercise; instead, it should be to reduce costs while enhancing stakeholder value. It should not impair the sales function or customer service levels, or in any other way negatively impact the organization. The two methods that we are going to discuss are well-known and popular techniques to reduce costs while enhancing operations. Now, let us discuss benchmarking in more detail.

What is benchmarking?

In this process, the business first identifies the applicable standards, and then takes steps to implement those standards or processes. Benchmarking helps in maintaining the correct perspective via internal appraisal and external analysis.

Benchmarking with respect to controlling costs can be defined as a process in which a business analyzes its operations to identify focus areas for cost control, and then identifies a standard against which the particular activity could be measured. Then, a plan can be created so that the standard can be achieved and continuously improved. The best practice or the standard should not always be measured in terms of the lowest costs, but it should enhance the overall value for all stakeholders.

> *Benchmarking is primarily the process of identifying the best practices or standards, and then applying them in order to reach the same level of effectiveness.*

At this point, we could define "who exactly the stakeholders are" to better understand the concept of benchmarking. A stakeholder is any party who has a "stake" or an interest with the company, business, or project. Usually, this includes the shareholders, the management, employees, customers, and suppliers.

Types of benchmarking

Internal benchmarking

Internal benchmarking relates to an analysis of existing practices of the business. You need to separately analyze various operating areas of the business to identify activities that could be enhanced or simplified while reducing costs. You also need to identify the drivers and what works well and why. Drivers are the triggers (for instance, a large customer order) that are likely to set in motion a series of events or activities. The key questions that need to be answered are:

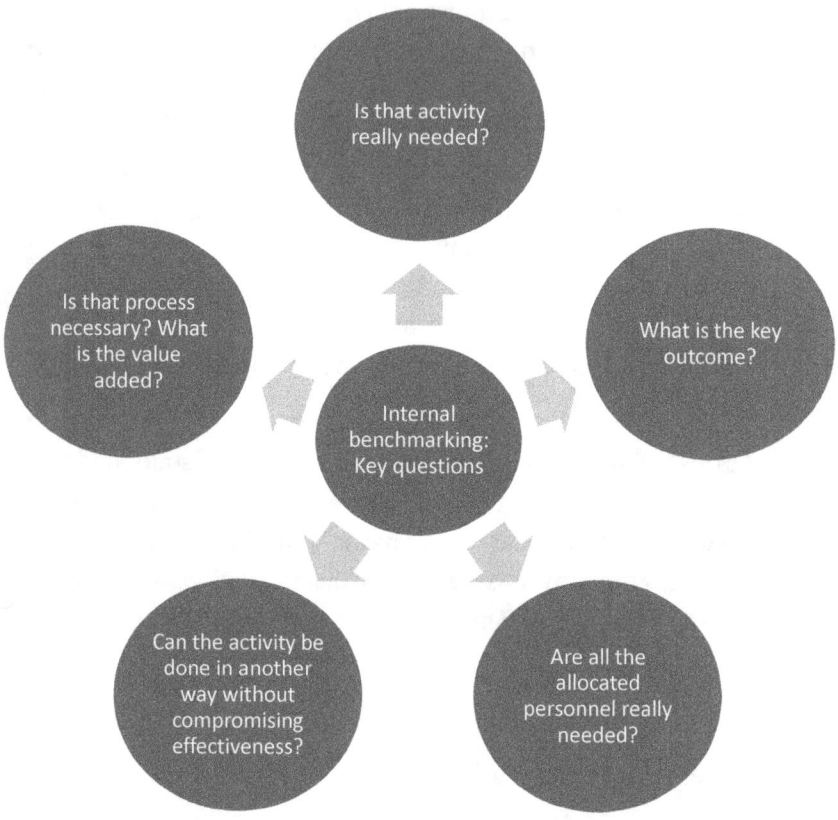

External benchmarking

External benchmarking primarily means a comparison of various aspects of the company's operations with operations of other companies. This could be helpful in developing objectives or focus areas for cost reduction and enhancing cash flow. External benchmarking could take three forms:

Competitive benchmarking:	Industry benchmarking:	Best-in-class benchmarking:
• In this type of benchmarking, a business tries to compare its own **key performance indicators (KPI)** with those of its competitors. In some cases, it might be difficult to find out a competitor's KPIs if its not a public company. But it could help by focusing on specific areas for improvement and to gain advantage over your competitors.	• Industry benchmarking tries to identify the latest industry trends, industry averages of the KPIs, and new innovations in the industry. This kind of identification could help in establishing standards that are accepted industry-wide and this could help in accelerating the company's growth.	• In this, we identify KPIs, best practices, as well as new and innovative practices, across a number of industries. If the benchmark is set at best practices, it supports continuous improvement, enhanced performance, and improvements in all operational areas of the company.

Benchmarking opportunities

<u>Comparing costs:</u> In its simplest form, benchmarking with the goal of controlling costs and enhancing cash flow would be to directly compare costs with the competitors. For instance, you could compare your utility bills or your personnel's remuneration against competitors or industry averages. If the costs are higher than the industry norms or the best practices, there may be an opportunity for savings.

<u>Comparing KPI':</u> Most commonly, while using benchmarking, companies compare KPIs, as these tend to focus on

enhancing the productivity and efficiency of the operations. Some KPIs are expressed quantitatively and, hence, are easier to measure such as profit margins, earnings per share, sales per employee, etc. Others are defined more qualitatively, such as effectiveness of marketing program or customer satisfaction level.

If any of the abovementioned KPIs indicate that the business is underperforming as compared to the chosen benchmark, this presents an opportunity to improve. For instance, if you choose the benchmark as the industry average and you realize that the gross profit margin for the industry is 25 percent while yours is only 15 percent, you might investigate where those extra costs are coming from, or if you could use cheaper materials without compromising the product quality.

<u>Comparing processes:</u> Benchmarking could be very helpful in comparing processes. This would include investigating in detail how other businesses carry out the same or similar processes, including the kind of technologies used or the type of production techniques or inventory management techniques employed. You could get some valuable ideas about how to apply those in your business.

Planning a benchmarking project

Typically, a benchmarking project could take 12 to 16 weeks to set up. However, if you do not plan to invest in external consultants, the only major cost would be the employee's work hours.

- You should set up a project team from various operational divisions of the business. However, a team of no more than five or six people is more likely to reach an agreement.
- The project will not be fruitful if the organization is not ready for change. You could organize training for key employees so that they can easily understand the benchmarking process and manage their teams.
- Identify the activities you want to benchmark or the KPIs, which, if benchmarked, would lead to the highest value creation for the stakeholders. It is advisable not to benchmark minor activities and only focus on main areas of your business.

Gathering data

To gather the data, you could approach the companies with whom you have decided to make comparisons ("partner companies"). You could use any existing contacts (if you are in the same business, it is possible that you share suppliers) to approach for the first time. You should explain the primary objectives of the study to the company and stress that mutual benefits could be derived.

The second step is the benchmarking agreement, and you can use a standard agreement. However, the agreement should include:

- The details of the information you need to exchange;
- How you plan to use that information;

- Who all will have access to the information; and
- The collection process and timeline.

It is necessary to have a focused approach for this research to derive the maximum benefits from the outcome.

The next step is to decide how to collect the data. Mainly, two approaches can be used:

- Questionnaire: using a questionnaire could collect operational data. You could send the questionnaire by post or email, or conduct a phone survey. This is the simplest data collection approach.
- Site visit: A site visit would give you a feel for the competition's operation.

Once the data collection is completed, you should send a copy of the findings to the partner company and get their comments on the findings. If the partner company has decided to conduct a similar exercise with you for information exchange, then their reports could also offer some insights to you about your business.

Managing the business enhancement

You should identify and summarize the key points where you differ from your benchmarking partner. Depending upon the objectives of the study, you may identify:

- Differences in KPIs: For instance, if you have higher staff turnover, lower sales to employee ratio, or lower gross margins.

- Differences in processes: For instance, your recruitment process could be more time-consuming or your sales reporting less efficient.

Once you have identified the differences, the next step is to investigate why you differ from the competition or the chosen benchmark. Usually, the reasons include: poor cost controls, inefficient or outdated processes, or you have traded off a certain KPI to enhance something else. Your focus could be different from that of your benchmarking partners or you are bound by budget or other constraints; for instance, you may not have the budget to invest in the latest technology.

Once you have identified the reasons for the differences between your performance and the benchmark, you need to decide the steps that could be taken to bridge that gap. There are three options:

- Do nothing: If there is a good reason for the difference and the cost of trying to bridge the gap is higher than the benefits sought, you can leave it as it is.
- Adapt your processes: If you feel that you could enhance your process and achieve better results, you may want to update your process as per the benchmarking partner's process.

- Target some areas and investigate further: This approach is chosen when you know that your process is underperforming compared to the competition, but it is not clear what the next steps should be to bridge the gap.

In conclusion, benchmarking could be an efficient and effective method for controlling costs in your organization. For any benchmarking project to be successful, you need to review and implement changes periodically – it is not a once-off activity. Regular updates are essential to remain up-to-date and achieve and maintain your competitive advantage.

In the next chapter, we will learn about the other most popular method to control costs in a business: activity-based costing.

KEY BUSINESS QUESTIONS

Current state

The answers to the following questions will allow you to analyze the current state of your operating cash outflows and might offer precious insights about ways to boost your cash flow.
- ✓ Do you feel the need to control costs in order to boost your cash flow?
- ✓ Do you currently have any organization-wide goals or benchmarks that are in process to be achieved?
- ✓ Have you, in the past 12 months, analyzed if your processes are at least as efficient as your competitor's

and if your KPIs are in line with industry averages?
- ✓ Are your various costs similar to what your competitors spend?

Six months from now

The answers to these questions would help you to gauge your progress in the past six months and will point out the most effective strategies.
- ✓ Did the benchmarking study achieve its objectives?
- ✓ What went well and what would you do differently next time?
- ✓ How well is your business performing now?
- ✓ Did the actions you took lead to incremental improvements or to a step change in performance?

Twelve months from now

The answers to these questions will help you to gauge your progress in the past 12 months.
- ✓ Do you have a process in place to review your benchmarks periodically?
- ✓ What would you like to do differently this time?
- ✓ How well is your business performing now?
- ✓ Did you reconsider the objectives of your benchmarking study with the changing external environment?

Cost Optimization: Activity-Based Costing

In the previous chapter, we understood that a dollar saved is a dollar worth of positive contribution to the cash flow. We also discussed, benchmarking as a tool of cost reduction and that it is an on-going initiative where once the benchmarks are set and achieved they should be periodically re-evaluated.

In this chapter, we will discuss **activity-based costing (ABC)** as a tool for cost reduction in a business. ABC does not replace the existing cost management methods in a company; rather, it is a once-off exercise. Using ABC helps management identify unnecessary or duplicated activities. It also helps in evaluating the benefit provided by the activities performed throughout the company.

After reading this chapter, you will be able to:

- ✓ Understand what activity-based costing is
- ✓ Understand the ABC process
- ✓ Be able to understand the ABC basics to control costs

What is activity-based costing?

In traditional costing methods, the business's overhead costs, such as electricity, marketing, etc., are allocated to each product or activity proportional to an activity's direct costs (such as the number of labor hours used for that activity). This is not suitable in every case as two activities that have the same

ABC identifies cost-saving opportunities

direct costs can use vastly different amounts of overhead costs

The main issue with the traditional costing approach is, if we reduce overhead costs in order to reduce the overall costs of the business, then it is similar to treating the symptoms and not the cause. In most cases, a simple reduction in overhead costs is likely to lead to a drop in the product quality and would still not reduce the costs for a longer term.

ABC's underlying assumption is totally different from that of traditional costing systems. Using ABC provides a business with a much more enhanced and accurate view of product cost. The cost allocation in ABC depends on the activities performed. In an ABC process, all the activities that are related to producing an item are determined and a cost is allocated to each activity. Thus, ABC assigns overhead costs on the basis of activities performed and those activities are identified as the cost drivers for overhead costs. As the actual cost drivers are determined, each activity is analyzed with respect to its necessity and scope. If it is determined that an activity is non-essential or could be performed via a more cost-effective method, and then it is eliminated or modified accordingly. As activities are modified or eliminated, the costs associated with them are also reduced or eliminated. These cost-savings directly impact the cash flow as well as the bottom line. However, ABC is usually used by businesses as a supplemental costing system. It could be done periodically to alter the system or process in order to make it more efficient, but in reducing the day-to-day overhead costs, benchmarking would be a better solution.

Application of activity-based costing

In ABC, at first a business needs to identify the overheads associated with each organizational activity. Then the costs of these activities are assigned to cost objects (products, services, or customers are referred to as cost objects as they are the basic cause behind an activity).

Steps involved in ABC:

1. Identify activities

    The company should analyze the operating processes of each department and identify the underlying activities. Usually each process would involve one or more activities.

2. Assign costs to activities

    This includes determining the cause of a cost occurrence and then tracing those costs to the associated cost objects. Costs could usually be of three types:

    - Direct costs – These are the costs that can be directly traced to one output, such as raw material costs.
    - Indirect costs – These are the costs that cannot be traced to a single output, for instance, maintenance costs.
    - Administrative costs – These are the costs that cannot be directly traced back to any product or service, for example, depreciation.

3. Identify outputs

    Identify all of the final outputs. An output is something for which an activity is being performed and, hence, resources are being consumed. Outputs could be products, services, or customers.

4. Assign activity costs to outputs

    Costs are assigned to the outputs based on the level of consumption of the activity or the demand for the activity for that specific output.

After assigning costs to activities, an in-depth analysis of each activity is required to determine whether or not the activity is essential. If it is essential, then an analysis is required to determine if it could be done at a lower cost without hampering the output quality.

ABC helps in improving the organization as well as the customer service. It could also help in reducing the costs and decreasing the cash conversion period. The focus should be to analyze all the activities, remove duplication, and enhance the remaining activities according to the industry best practices.

In an ABC process, you should look at the following:

Products/services	• To continue or discontinue, expand the production or contract, expand the product line, cost and profit considerations, break-even analysis
Customers	• Analysis of current and potential clients, customer service considerations, how profitable a customer is, historical statistics (revenue, costs, and profits), and forecasts
Activities	• In-depth analysis of all activities along with the value they create for the business, including those that support the business at additional cost, but provide no direct value to the outputs, such as administrative services and other support functions.
Indicators of poor performance	• Special emphasis should be given to the operational measures that indicate if there is scope, such as customer returns and rejects

Uses of ABC

ABC is widely accepted as a comprehensive companywide performance measurement system that supports a range of improvements such as:

- <u>Cost performance measurement:</u> Identifying opportunities for reducing costs, improving quality and processes, and so on.

- Analyzing cost performance: Identifying the overhead costs and correctly assigning it to a specific output; this can lead to insights about economy and efficiency improvements. It can also lead to certain strategic insights about product pricing and efficiency.

- Process improvements: As it sheds light on all the essential and non-essential activities, it could help in an analysis of operating methods and processes, use of equipment, productivity of personnel, customer relations, inefficiencies, waste elimination, etc.

- Organizational management: It allows the top management to operate the business in an optimum cost-versus-benefit manner.

- Cash management: Helps in identifying areas for reduction and the elimination of unnecessary costs; pricing strategies that maximize top line and bottom line.

Let's look at an example of Judy's Products Ltd. to understand how ABC can help a business to identify correct strategies. The following are the allocated costs for two of the company's products by traditional and activity-based costing methods.

Traditional costing

Product name	Total Units	Raw material costs	Labor cost	Overhead costs	Total cost	Cost/Unit	Selling price
AA	40	120	100	200	420	10.5	14
BB	100	360	500	1,000	1,860	18.6	24

Activity-based costing

Product name	Total Units	Raw material costs	Labor cost	Unit activity	Batch activity	Product line activity	Total Cost	Cost/ Unit	Selling price
AA	40	120	100	100	50	350	720	18	-
BB	100	360	500	30	80	400	1370	13.7	24

We see in the tables above that, by correctly allocating costs, we realize that Product AA has a selling price of $14, but its cost per unit is actually $18; hence, the company cannot make money by selling it at the current selling price.

Let us take another example to clarify the concept. Let us assume a production company has heavy expenditures for research and development (R&D). The company produces two products, product A and product B. In this example, we see that product B uses much more R&D initiatives than product A; however, as the direct labor cost is higher for product A, it has higher overheads using the traditional costing method. Using ABC, we get a much clearer picture of the actual use of overhead costs.

	Product A	Product B	Total
Total Production Volume	2,000	1,000	
Cost per R&D Initiative	1,000	1,000	
Number of R&D Initiatives	5	10	
Total cost of R&D Initiatives	5,000	10,000	15,000
Direct labor hours/unit produced	5	2	
Direct labor hours	10,000	2,000	12,000
R&D Initiatives cost for direct labor per hr ($15,000/12,000)			1.25
ABC overhead cost/unit (A = $5,000/2,000; B = $10,000/10,000)	2.5	10	
Conventional overhead cost/ unit (A = $1.25 x 5 direct labor hours; B = $1.25 x 2 direct labor hours)	7.5	5	

By using the ABC concepts, where overhead activities and the associated costs are assigned to the outputs based on consumption of the activity, costs are calculated more accurately. The company's management would need to decide about the future of this product after looking at the ABC data. The company could decide to stop selling it, increase its selling price, or reduce the costs by modifying activities.

In conclusion, the operational costs of a business are the majority of the cash outflows. Thus, to enhance cash flow, it is necessary for the business to control these costs. While cost control is a fairly effective way for a business to enhance profitability, most small business owners do not fully understand the impact of cost control on cash flow.

Benchmarking as well as activity-based costing are two effective methods to ensure better-cost control for a business. Benchmarking helps the company to compare its costs and processes with industry best practices, which have already been proven to work well. ABC is a more customized method of cost analysis for a company to determine its cost drivers and allocate costs more efficiently. In this chapter, we have attempted to explain the basics of activity-based costing and the underlying principles of ABC should allow a business to enhance its processes for long-term cost control.

KEY BUSINESS QUESTIONS

Current state

The answers to the following questions will allow you to analyze the current state of your cash flows and might offer precious insights about your business. If the answer to any of the following questions is yes, an ABC analysis could help you to reduce costs and optimize your processes:

- ✓ Are you able to maintain optimum inventories (raw material, work-in-process, finished goods), that is, minimize storage costs while being able to fulfil urgent orders?
- ✓ Do you feel you need to lower product costs to meet your future cash flow needs effectively?
- ✓ Do you feel smaller manufacturing lots could help you save costs?
- ✓ Do you agree that building quality into the process rather than having it, as an add-on process will help you to enhance efficiency?
- ✓ Are the staff and equipment productivity at optimum?
- ✓ Do you often face dissatisfied customers due to defective/wrong deliveries?
- ✓ Do you need to identify value-added cost elements to enhance quality?
- ✓ Do you need to control costs of nonproduction-related activities?

Six months from now

The answers to these questions will help you to gauge your progress in the past six months and will point out the most effective strategies.

- ✓ Did you undertake an ABC initiative?

- ✓ Do you plan to monitor the performance enhancements?
- ✓ Was your key sales staffing part of the process?
- ✓ What benefits did you notice by undertaking the ABC initiative?
- ✓ How much has the cash flow improved in the past six months? What strategies have contributed most to the improvement?

Twelve months from now

The answers to these questions will help you to gauge your progress in the past 12 months.

- ✓ Did you revisit your ABC initiative and measure the progress caused by last year's initiative?
- ✓ What were the potential benefits of undertaking the initiative again? Have your processes significantly changed after the last ABC initiative?
- ✓ How much has the cash flow improved in the past 12 months? What strategies have contributed most to the improvement?

Cash Flow Management: Finance Function

In this chapter, we will discuss the contribution of the finance function in cash management for a small business. We will cover the three main activities to be handled by the finance function, in terms of cash management, which are: **Investing**, **Financing**, and **Borrowing**.

After reading this chapter, you will be able to:

- ✓ Understand the function of the finance division in cash management
- ✓ Understand the basics of creating a short-term investment policy
- ✓ Understand how to evaluate long-term investments
- ✓ Understand the various sources of borrowing cash in terms of a shortfall

One of the most important components of successful cash management is putting the surplus money to use (i.e., to invest the money in a way that it earns for the business in a protective manner). If the finance function were not able to invest the money properly, then all the other cash management systems that are in place in the company would lose some of their advantages. Apart from investing excess cash, the second most important job for the finance function would be to cover the shortfall, if and when it happens, either by financing or borrowing.

Funding the shortfall, when needed, requires careful planning and forecasting. It is difficult to borrow from a bank if the company is in a cash crisis. It is much easier if you have planned and forecasted your requirements beforehand and avoided a crisis situation. Acquisition of long-term funding is even more difficult than getting short-term funding as it needs a higher and deeper level of planning. Deciding whether to issue new equity or bonds or any form of long-term financing takes considerable time; hence, this option is not available at the time of a crisis. Thus, the most important part of overall cash management for a small business is deciding and planning how to acquire funds in case of a shortfall to keep the company going.

Investing

It is of utmost importance to have a proper investment policy in place before any small company starts investing its surplus cash. This helps in aligning the finance function and investments with the long-term goals and strategies of the company.

The major points that should be included in the investment policy for investing its excess cash for the short-term are:

Company's short-term investment goal: This is important and usually depends on the amount of excess cash available and the forecasts regarding expected cash needs. A company's short-term investment goal could be to maintain liquidity for immediate needs, maximizing gains, or just principal maintenance.

The company's risk-taking capacity: Similar to the investment goals, the company's risk threshold also usually depends on the amount of cash

Create a sound investment policy before starting investments

availability. For instance, the company needs to decide if an aggressive investment strategy is more suitable to maximize gains or if a conservative approach with higher liquidity is preferable.

Investment restrictions: Many companies have some investment restrictions for ethical reasons or it is bound by some loan covenants. This needs to be clearly specified in the policy.

Diversification of assets: For investments, especially for short-term investments, it is very important to decide the diversification requirement of the funds. What should be the division of funds among risky and non-risky assets? What amount of funds needs to be in highly liquid assets? These are crucial questions that need to be answered in the investment policy.

Investment audits: There should be audit schedules and procedures in place. Also, it should be ensured that proper controls are maintained so that the policies are followed.

Evaluating short-term investment opportunities

To evaluate short-term opportunities, we need to consider a number of factors such as yield, return on investment (ROI), or risk issues. The investment strategy's objective should be to follow the investment policy and maximize investment yield in tandem with the company's attitude toward risk and liquidity.

To evaluate the various investment instruments available in the market, there are certain basic guidelines to consider, these are:

Investment Quality	• Safer investments are said to be higher quality investments, though they have lower yields. Investments with higher risks are likely to have higher yields.
Price volatility	• Investments that have a volatile market price are considered higher risk investments. Conversely, an instrument with low price volatility is likely to be less risky.
Liquidity	• Highly liquid investments are highly marketable but have lower yields. Higher yields can usually be attained at a higher risk with reduced marketability and, hence, reduced liquidity.
Maturity date	• Generally, if an instrument has a late maturity date, it has higher yield in order to compensate for the longer period of risk and vice versa.
Return on Investment	• It is the most important factor to be considered before investing and depends on the abovementioned factors.

Evaluation of long-term investment opportunities

Apart from short-term investment decisions, a company has to decide on many long-term projects which need significant financial resources, such as enhancing plant capacity, buying new equipment, long-term financial investments, etc.

There are a number of established methods in place to evaluate such long-term capital investments. In this section, we will discuss a few of them in brief.

Discounted cash flow method

Discounted cash flow (DCF) is an approach used for evaluating the viability of a capital investment project in terms of cash flow. In this, we analyze future cash flows in terms of their worth today. This method uses discounting, which is the opposite of compounding. This DCF approach discounts future cash flows to their present value, based on an applicable discount (interest) rate. Let's understand it using an example. If you are receiving $200,000 in four years' time and the discount rate is 10 percent, then in today's terms, the cash value would be calculated as follows:

> At end of year 4 = $4,000
> Start of year 4= $4,000/1.1 = $3,636.36
> Start of year 3 = $3,636.36/1.1 = $3,305.08
> Start of year 2= $3,305/1.1 = $3,005.25
> Today = $3005.25/1.1 = $2732.05

Capital investment strategies should be based on the measurement of cash flows, instead of profits and losses. Some cash flow factors to consider include:

- ✓ Incremental cash flows: Only those cash flows should be included in the calculations, which are a direct result of the capital investment strategy.

- ✓ Residual values: Estimate the salvage value of the project at the end of the project life. Often, the sale value at the end of the project makes a huge difference between a good and a bad deal.

- ✓ Depreciation: Depreciation is a non-cash expense so depreciation itself is not considered in the DCF calculations; however, the tax savings resulting from the depreciation should be considered as part of the positive cash flow.

- ✓ Tax considerations: Tax laws applicable to capital investments have a direct impact on the project's cash flows and, hence, should be considered in evaluating the viability of a project.

Net present value

The **net present value (NPV)** approach is a DCF technique that takes the time value of money into account. The NPV approach calculates the present value of the cash inflows and compares them to the present value of the cash outflows at a certain discount rate. This discount rate could either be the company's cost of capital or a minimum acceptable rate of return needed for the investment. The NPV is primarily the difference between the present value of the cash inflows and cash outflows. If the NPV is positive, then the capital investment is acceptable. If the NPV is negative, the capital project is usually deemed unacceptable.

Internal rate of return

The **internal rate of return (IRR)** is a capital investment evaluation approach that ascertains the actual rate of return on a proposed capital investment project taking into account the time value of money. This method is somewhat similar to the NPV approach, but the difference is that it determines the actual rate of return being generated by the project. The actual rate of return that is calculated using this method can then be analyzed to decide if the project return is acceptable.

Financing sources for the business

As we have understood, one of the main responsibilities for a company's finance function is to ensure that sufficient funds are available to meet the business's needs. This issue is important for virtually all aspects of a business and is often a survival issue for many small businesses.

Developing a cash flow forecast provides answers regarding the affordability of capital investment projects and requires immense planning and budgeting. Once it is concluded that the company's plan would not be satisfied with in-house funds, and then it is required to plan for acquisition of the rest of the funds. Some of common sources of funding are:

- Profits: The most preferable sources of funds; however, it is important that the profits convert into cash inflow for the company for it to be a viable source of funds for capital investments.

- Sale of assets: Redundant assets could be liquidated to get additional cash resources if needed and if possible. However, this form of obtaining funds should not be relied upon, as it is possible that a business can do serious harm to itself if this is done without a proper decision-making process.

• <u>New equity</u>: Generally, privately held small businesses are not able to acquire new equity funds easily. There are numerous issues related to control and liquidity, which could make new equity acquisition problematic. For publicly held companies, raising new equity capital is feasible, but needs considerable planning due to the related expense, the dilution of ownership issues.

• <u>Borrowing</u>: Apart from retained earnings, borrowing is the most popular source of capital for small businesses. For a well-managed, planned, and profitable business, borrowing is usually the cheapest source of funds. There are a number of sources available to businesses for borrowing and by funds can be obtained on a short- or longer-term basis.

Borrowing sources

There are numerous alternatives for a business that is profitable and is managed well for borrowing money, these are:

Banks: It is usually preferable to borrow money from the company's own bank as the bank knows the company's business and is best-informed about the company's suitability for a loan. The company could borrow in the form of a line of credit, demand loans, or a cash overdraft. Most commonly, if collateral is required, it could be accounts receivable.

Life insurance companies: Loans from life insurance companies are usually not suitable for the shorter term and, hence, are only suitable if the funds are needed for a longer term.

Investment brokers: A company can borrow from investment brokers with the securities held as collateral for short-term borrowings.

Accounts receivable financing: Accounts receivable can be sold to a factoring company at approximately 80 percent of the face value.

Inventory financing: A small business could also borrow money using its inventory as collateral. Generally, such borrowing is suitable for the shorter term.

Customers and suppliers: There are times it is possible to borrow from customers via advances against orders or early payment of accounts receivable. Supplier financing is likely to be easier, since the supplier gets to make a sale and financing could be considered part of the pricing arrangement through extended payment, sale in installments, or leasing.

KEY BUSINESS QUESTIONS

Current state

The answers to the following questions will allow you to analyze the current state of your cash flow policies and might offer precious insights about your business. These questions could help the company in creating a sound investment policy that suits its long-term strategy.

- ✓ What is the business's short-term investment goal?
- ✓ What is the risk tolerance threshold of the business (i.e., the level of risk a company is willing to assume)?
- ✓ Are there any investment restrictions for the company?
- ✓ Who is responsible for investment activities?
- ✓ What is the level of diversification that is applied to the investments?
- ✓ Does the company have an established audit program for its investments?

Six months from now

The answers to these questions will help you to gauge your progress in the past six months and will point out the most effective strategies.

- ✓ Did you create an investment policy?
- ✓ Do you plan to monitor the performance of the investments?
- ✓ What benefits did you notice by creating an investment policy?
- ✓ How much has the cash flow improved in the past six months? What strategies have contributed most to the improvement?

Twelve months from now

The answers to these questions will help you to gauge your progress in the past 12 months.

- ✓ Did you revisit your investment policy and measure the progress caused by last year's initiative?
- ✓ What were the potential benefits of undertaking the initiative again?
- ✓ How much has the cash flow improved in the past 12 months? What strategies have contributed most to the improvement?

Forecasting Cash Flow for Future Periods

Up to now, we have learned the importance of having internal systems to manage cash transactions and cash balances. In this chapter, we will understand the advantages of knowing the expected cash flows in advance. By planning for future cash flows, the company can avoid surprises and possible crisis situations. The primary focus of cash flow planning is to have future expected cash inflows exceed cash outflows and take essential steps to sustain positive cash flow. A comparison and analysis of planned and actual results equips us with information necessary for well-informed decision-making and enhanced future planning.

In order to plan for future cash flow with reasonable accuracy, it is important to take into account the company's past actual cash flows. At the very minimum, the past 12 months (if not longer) of cash flows must be studied and reviewed in detail and used as the basis of future projections.

Forecasting cash

Forecasting the company's cash gives us an idea about what to expect in the future, and whether the company is likely to face a cash shortfall or cash excess. This allows for planning strategies to cover the gap in shortfall or investing excess cash accordingly. The difference between cash forecasting and planning is that forecasting is the projection of the most likely financial position in the future. Whereas cash planning involves creating strategies and action plans based on the forecasts. Thus, though forecasting is the first step, cash planning is the primary focus for cash management of a company.

Planning

The company should focus on creating both short-term and long-term plans. Short-term plans are usually for up to a year and long-term plans could be of any length for which you can reasonably plan. It is also beneficial to indulge in scenario planning with projections that are based on best case, worst case, and most likely scenarios. For instance, your business could be significantly impacted by currency fluctuations, economic growth, or changes in interest rate. Planning beforehand for likely future scenarios is likely to help in assessing a range of possibilities and plans to cope with each of them. You just need to ensure a level of flexibility in planning so that the strategies can be adjusted based on the changing business environment.

The focus of any cash flow planning exercise should be on the following:

- Stabilizing cash flow: For most companies, cash flow varies considerably from one period to the next. This makes the current strategies obsolete for the next period and significant fluctuations also make it difficult to plan. Having a better idea about prospective cash shortfalls or excesses is likely to help the company in planning accordingly.
- Invest the excess cash at the earliest: It is not prudent to leave the cash idle when it could be put to work for the business in an interest-bearing account and contribute to enhancing overall return for the business.

Effective cash planning may make it feasible for the company to make investments earlier to generate maximum returns from excess cash.
- <u>Deferring borrowings:</u> With effective cash flow planning, we can estimate if a cash shortfall is likely to occur. However, having this information in advance gives us the opportunity to look for other methods to cover the cash gap, instead of borrowing. This leads to delaying the borrowing as much as possible and, hence, helps with savings on interest charges. Without a plan in place, if a company has to raise cash urgently, it is also likely to pay a higher rate of interest.

Steps in cash flow planning

The cash flow planning essentially consists of the following steps:

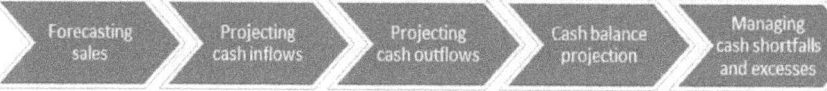

<u>Forecasting sales</u>

The sales forecast forms the basis of cash flow planning. The level of accuracy of the sales forecast would directly impact the cash flow plan. The sales forecast estimates the sales in any given period and then estimate the cash inflows accordingly. The expected sales levels also form the basis for projected cash outflows for the period. The sales forecast is created on the basis of the expected customer orders and its accuracy would make the cash budget more accurate.

Projecting cash inflows

The actual cash inflow in a company does not occur from "sales" unless it is a cash sale; it occurs when accounts receivables are collected. If a company has a stable average collection period, then cash inflow is likely to be directly proportional to the sales volume. However, for most small companies, there is no stability in sales and collections.

A reliable cash inflow projection requires meticulous analysis of accounts receivable collection patterns in the past with reasonable assumptions for the future to determine as precisely as possible the delay in actual cash inflow after the sale occurrence. The company's historical cash collection pattern can be ascertained by analyzing historical cash inflows with respect to sales, and the collection pattern translates into the assumptions to be used for future projections.

As discussed in "Managing inflows", if a company is equipped with the historical collection patterns information, coupled with the past payment patterns of specific customers, the company could decide which customers are paying early and which could be offered discounts as an incentive to expedite cash payments. The company could also introduce differential pricing with lower prices for timely paying customers and higher prices for late paying customers. Differential pricing is also likely to act as an incentive for the customers to pay.

Projecting cash outflows

Cash outflows could be categorized into three main categories:

- Cash outflows for purchases such as inventory and long-term assets
- Cash outflows for operating expenses
- Debt servicing, including interest payments, principal repayments, and dividends

If the sales forecast is fairly accurate, then it is much simpler to forecast the future expenses. The sales forecast forms the foundation and the company is likely to spend on inventory and operating expenses depending on the level of expected sales. You could gather historical data for your company and use a five-year or three-year average expenditure as a percentage of your sales for future projections. Debt repayment is usually known at the start of the period and, hence, it is easy to be included in the forecast.

A cash outflow projection allows for introspection about the company's expense levels and these could be reviewed for their validity using the following questions:

- Purchases: What is the direct inventory or product costs as a percentage of sales? Is it at an optimum level? Could it be reduced?
- Salaries: Is it possible to reduce this expense by outsourcing or temporary staff? Could the non-value added positions be eliminated?
- Sales commissions: Is this the best method to incentivize your sales staff? Is the level of commission optimum to maintain staff motivation and enhance the top line?
- Debt: Will it be beneficial to use excess funds to reduce debt as compared to paying interest for a longer term?

Were the funds raised via borrowing put to optimum use?
- Sales, general and administrative expenses: Which ones are necessary? Which could be reduced or eliminated?

Cash balance projection

After we have determined the expected cash inflows and outflows, the next step is to calculate the net impact on the company's cash balances. It is prudent to show the net cash flow for each period and then cumulatively. This would provide a clear picture of whether a shortfall is likely to occur in a month.

Let us understand the forecasting process with the help of an example:

We have a company with two products, product A and product B. According to historical data, we know that product A's sales increase at a rate of 25 percent per year and product B's sales increase at a rate of 10 percent per year. The company is likely to sell 1,000 units per month of product A in year one of the sales forecasts at a price of $5. For product B, the company is likely to sell 500 units per month in year one at a price of $40.

For product A, the direct costs are estimated to be 20 percent of the sales and the percentage is assumed to be constant for the forecast periods. For product B, the direct costs are 15 percent of the sales.

So for year one, we sell 12,000 units (12 x 1,000) of product A at $5; hence the revenue generated would be $60,000 and would increase at a rate of 25 percent in year one and year two.

Similarly, the sales forecast for product B is also created.

	Year 1	Year 2	Year 3
Sales			
Product A	$60,000	$75,000	$93,750
Product B	$240,000	$264,000	$290,400
Total Revenue	$300,000	$339,000	$384,150
Direct Cost			
Product A	$12,000	$15,000	$18,750
Product B	$36,000	$39,600	$43,560
Total Direct Cost	$48,000	$54,600	$62,310
Gross Margin	$252,000	$284,400	$321,840
Gross Margin %	84%	84%	84%

According to historical data, the following would be the cash flow assumptions used:

Table 4: Cash Flow Assumptions.

Cash Inflow	
% Of Sales on Credit	80%
Avg Collection Period (Days)	45
Cash Outflow	
% Of Purchases on Credit	70%

Avg Payment Delay (Days)	60
Inventory	
Months to Keep on Hand	2
Minimum Inventory Purchase	$5,000

The company's expenses are forecasted as follows:

The company has three employees with a total salary of $90,000 per year and it is estimated to increase at a rate of 10 percent per year. Employee-related expenses are assumed to be 10 percent of the total yearly salary. Rent is $1,500 per month and is likely to remain stable for the foreseeable future due to lease agreements in place. Utilities, office supplies, and insurance are estimated based on historical charges. Marketing and promotion charges are estimated to be 5 percent of the sales. The company is planning to buy additional equipment costing $20,000 in month six of the forecast and there are no other additional asset purchases likely to occur in the forecast period.

Table 5: Company's Expenses.

	Year 1	Year 2	Year 3
Operating Expenses			
Salary	$90,000	$99,000	$108,900
Employee-Related Expenses	$9,000	$9,900	$10,890
Marketing & Promotions	$15,000	$16,950	$19,207
Rent	$18,000	$18,000	$18,000
Utilities	$6,000	$6,000	$6,000
Office Supplies	$1,000	$1,000	$1,000
Insurance	$1,000	$1,000	$1,000
Total Operating Expenses	**$140,000**	**$151,850**	**$164,997**
Major Purchases			
Equipment	$20,000	$0	$0
Total Major Purchases	**$20,000**	**$0**	**$0**

We receive an equity input of $30,000 at the start of the forecast period and a debt input of $20,000 at a rate of 7 percent for 60 months. We arrive at the following cash flow statement:

Table 6: Cash Flow Statement.

	Year 1	Year 2	Year 3
Operations			
Net Profit	$96,543	$113,465	$135,323
Depreciation and Amortization	$2,333	$4,000	$4,000
Change in Accounts Receivable	($30,000)	($3,900)	($4,518)
Change in Inventory	($14,000)	($400)	$2,310
Change in Accounts Payable	$11,785	$228	$263
Change in Sales Taxes Payable	$0	$0	$0
Net Cash Flow from Operations	**$66,661**	**$113,393**	**$137,378**
Investing & Financing			
Assets Purchased or Sold	($20,000)	$0	$0
Investments Received	$30,000	$0	$0
Change in Short-Term Debt	$0	$0	$0
Change in Long-Term Debt	$16,836	($3,691)	($3,957)
Net Cash Flow from Investing & Financing	**$26,836**	**($3,691)**	**($3,957)**
Cash at Beginning of Period	$0	$93,497	$203,199
Net Change in Cash	$93,497	$109,702	$133,421
Cash at End of Period	**$93,497**	**$203,199**	**$336,620**

Managing cash surplus and shortfalls

A company needs to manage a suitable amount of cash reserve, and until the time the cash position falls below that reserve, there is little cause for alarm. If the cash position is considerably above the cash reserve, then the company needs to plan investments, as in the abovementioned example. We see in Table 6 that the company is likely to enhance its cash reserves every year and, hence, could plan to invest the excess idle cash.

However, if the forecast shows that the cash reserve is likely to be depleted, the company could plan some actions such as delaying the payables, accelerating the receivables, or raising some extra cash via debt or equity injection.

In conclusion, cash flow planning is an integral part of managing a company's finances. With cash flow planning, a company could mitigate risks and plan strategies to handle any shortfalls or excesses.

Identifying the cash reserve that needs to be maintained is also an essential part of cash flow planning and requires careful analysis. Without sufficient planning, the company is likely to keep the excess cash idle longer than necessary and, on the contrary, in the event of a shortfall, the company would not have sufficient time to come up with suitable strategies. Hence, for a small business, even if it seems like a waste of resources initially, on the whole, it will be highly beneficial for the company to invest time and resources in cash flow planning.

KEY BUSINESS QUESTIONS

Current state

The answers to the following questions will allow you to analyze the current state of your cash flows and might offer precious insights about ways to boost your cash flow in future.

- ✓ Do you create a sales forecast and cash flow forecast?
- ✓ Could you answer the following critical questions for your business:
  - Are you making sales to the right customers, thus avoiding late payments and bad debts?
  - Is your payment terms suitable for your cash flow needs?
  - Is the collection period well within the industry average?
  - Is the amount of collections that occur beyond the company's terms (e.g., net 30 days) high?
  - What are the direct inventory or product costs as a percentage of sales? Is it at an optimum level? Could it be reduced?
  - Is it possible to reduce this expense by outsourcing or temporary staff? Could the non-value added positions be eliminated?
  - Is this the best method to incentivize your sales staff? Is the level of commission optimum to maintain staff motivation and enhance the top line?
  - Will it be beneficial to use excess funds to reduce debt as compared to paying interest for a longer term? Were the funds raised via borrowing put to optimum use?

- Sales, general, and administrative expenses:
- Which ones are necessary? Which could be reduced or eliminated?

- ✓ Do you have a set amount identified to be kept as a cash reserve
- ✓ Do you often face cash shortfalls?
- ✓ Are you able to invest your excess funds properly in case of surplus cash?

Six months from now

The answers to these questions would help you to gauge your progress in the past six months and would point out the most effective strategies.

- ✓ Did you create a process for making sales forecasts and cash plans?
- ✓ Do you plan to monitor the plan's performance with respect to the plan?
- ✓ Was there considerable difference between the planned and actual result in the past six months?
- ✓ Are you able to identify the reasons for these differences?
- ✓ What benefits did you notice by having a cash plan ready?
- ✓ How much has the cash flow improved in the past six months? What strategies have contributed most to the improvement?

Twelve months from now

The answers to these questions will help you to gauge your

progress in the past 12 months.

- ✓ Did you create a process for making sales forecasts and cash plans?
- ✓ Do you plan to monitor the plan's performance with respect to the plan?
- ✓ Was there considerable difference between the planned and actual result in the past 12 months?
- ✓ Are you able to identify the reasons for these differences?
- ✓ What benefits did you notice by having a cash plan ready?
- ✓ How much has the cash flow improved in the past 12 months? What strategies have contributed most to the improvement?

Cash Flow: Analyze Actuals vs Forecast

Up to now, we have learned about the operational aspects of cash flow management and forecasting and being prepared for likely future situations. In this chapter, we will learn about cash flow analysis and control, which is as important as profit analysis or cost analysis for companies in this dynamic business environment.

After reading this chapter, you will be able to:

- ✓ Understand the advantages of cash flow analysis and control
- ✓ Understand the components of a cash flow statement
- ✓ Understand the use of ratio analysis for cash flow analysis

Cash flow reporting and analysis

If you have developed a cash flow planning system, then it is relatively simple to report the actual cash flows as the system is already in place. The cash flow reports of actual results are generated by the accounting team; thus, it is only a matter of keeping records of actual cash flows, and reporting in an acceptable format, ideally the same format as the planning system is using as it would make the comparison and analysis easier.

Monthly reporting and control could avoid crisis

The frequency of the generation of actual reports differs from company to company, but it is advisable to generate these at least monthly and compare and contrast the monthly report with the forecasted figures. The comparison would be straightforward if you are forecasting for months. If you are forecasting for quarters instead of months, then you could compare the monthly reports with one-third of the quarterly projections. This would give you an idea if you are falling behind your forecasted figures in a given month so that you can take steps to cover the gap in the following months.

Controlling cash flow usually has the following steps:

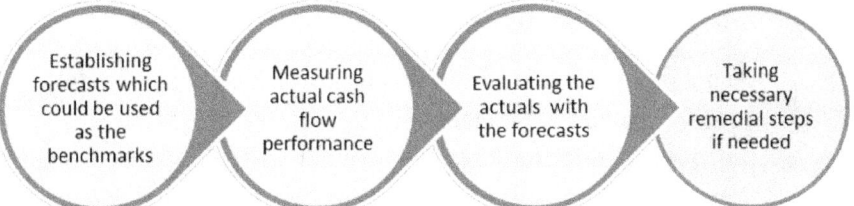

The first step in this process is to establish the standard to which we will compare the actual results. This is done in the cash flow planning process, when we forecast and plan for the likely results and goal to be achieved. Hence, the outcome of the cash planning exercise gives us the benchmark to which we could compare the actual results.

Performance measurement is done by generating the cash flow reports as discussed earlier. The evaluation phase, in general, does not have any set procedure; hence, any measure of financial performance, which is important for the business in the current scenarios, could be used. It could be cost variance, variance in expected return on investment, or a variance in the cash position between the actual and the forecasts.

The final step is to take necessary remedial steps, if needed. If there is a considerable difference between the forecast and the actuals, then you need to find the reason for the gap and explore the root cause. Understanding the underlying cause could help to avoid the same in the future. Hence, by using monthly reporting and control you might still have time to reach your quarterly or yearly cash goal.

Analyzing the statement of cash flows

To make any kind of sound business decision based on data analysis, we need data from multiple time periods for a thorough evaluation. This is true when analyzing the cash flow statements as well. Mainly, this is because month over month fluctuations are quite common in cash flows and are highly dependent on other parties. For instance, in one month a company might get cash inflow of x dollars, but in the next month it might get an inflow of 3x dollars due to a number of reasons that could be affecting the customers. A single period might have certain uncommonly occurring events and, hence, it could not be taken as representative of normal business activity. Hence, any business owner needs to review cash flows for multiple periods to make sound judgments regarding the performance of the business in the aspect of cash flow.

Ideally, you should use the historical data from three to five years so that you can do a trend analysis. A more extensive analysis could be done using more than five years of data, but it is not advisable to use more than 10 years of historical data because it is likely to be outdated and not be of much of use.

The cash flow statement has three segments:

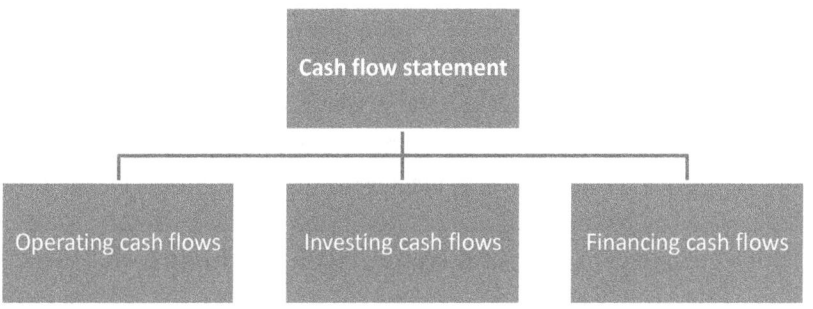

Each part of the cash flow statement needs to be reviewed separately as these are impacted by different business activities.

Cash flow from operating activities

In the cash flow, the most important section that needs to be reviewed is the operating cash flows, as this is the most important source of funds for a business. The most important source of cash for any business is its profits. Generating profits is the reason any company is in business. Hence, for most cases, if a company's main source of cash is not its operating cash flows, it is not likely to survive for much longer. Borrowing, financing, and capital gains are all sources of cash, but these are the supplemental sources rather than the main source. These can be used at any point if needed to generate cash, but these cannot be the main source of a company's cash over a longer period of time.

Now, if we consider a company's profits, we know that there are a number of non-cash charges, which significantly impact the level of profits a company generates, such as depreciation, change in accounts receivable, etc. These should be added back to the profit to determine the actual amount of operating cash. There are many extraordinary items, such as capital gains, lawsuit settlements, etc., which need to be individually evaluated for a period when we are analyzing the cash flow statements for multiple periods so that we are not comparing apples to oranges. Evaluating the extraordinary items and other one-time charges gives us the normalized statements, which are fit for comparison, so that we get a genuine trend and, hence, appropriate conclusions to the analysis.

Cash flow from investing activities

From the cash flow perspective, investing activities include all major purchases for the business, such as property, plants, and equipment. Purchase of these long-term assets will reduce cash and the sale of any such asset will add cash (if the sale has occurred on a cash basis). New business acquisitions would also be included in this category as it is the company's investment in its own future.

The company should take steps to reinvest in its future at regular intervals as the initial long-term assets depreciate with time. Hence, reinvestment would help in maintaining the company's asset base. However, reinvestment should not be done just for the sake of reinvestment and it should be reviewed carefully so that it helps a company's growth.

Cash flow from financing activities

The review of this section tells us how effectively the business is able to serve its debt and other obligations. If the company is borrowing too much for long periods then it could cause problems with servicing the debt in future. When a company's debt is too low compared to the equity, it could indicate that the management is too conservative and the company could lose out on the benefits of leverage.

Occasionally, a company is likely to see a change in capital structure. Though such a change has a considerable impact on the cash and financial position of the company, these changes are so infrequent that they usually do not impact the cash flows on a regular basis.

Hence, we see that in a business, the primary source of cash generation is operational cash flow and the generated cash is used for investing activities. Financing cash is generally a varying number, which balances the other two cash flows; for instance, in the case of a shortfall, cash could be raised using financing activities. To determine the optimum cash goals and an optimum investment plan, the company needs to analyze its historical data and come up with goals after adjusting for changes in

> *Ratio analysis is used to express relationships between a firm's finances and the trends over time that could evaluate*

the business scenario.

Ratio analysis

Ratio analysis is a simple yet effective tool to analyze a company's cash flow statement. A company should consider its operational and financial position to understand the best ratios needed to evaluate its cash flow. Acceptable results depend on a number of factors and, hence, are likely to vary from company to company.

The table below gives a list of ratios that could be useful for analyzing the company's cash flow. However, you must keep in mind that there are a number of additional ratios that could be used. What is important is to determine which of the ratios are important and most significant for the company.

Ratio	Description	Formula
Cash to profit ratio.	The ratio indicates the percentage of operating profit that has been converted into cash—a measure of cash conversion	Operating cash flows/ Operating income
Cash sales to total sales.	The amount of sales immediately converted into cash—a cash efficiency measure.	Cash sales/ Total sales
Reinvestment ratio.	The amount of operating cash flows used for capital expenditures—a measure of the degree of capital reinvestment	Purchase of property, plant and equipment/ Operating cash flows
Debt payoff.	The amount of operating cash flows used to pay off debt	Debt payments/ Operating cash flows
Cash return on assets.	The amount of cash generated from total asset investment in the business—a cash return on investment (ROI) measure	Operating cash flows/Total assets
Cash return on equity.	An ROI measure of cash return on stockholder's equity	Operating cash flows/ Stockholder' equity
Cash return on capital employed.	An ROI measure of cash return on capital employed in the business	Operating cash flows/Capital employed
Cash flow current ratio.	Ability of cash generated from operations to cover current liabilities	Operating cash flows/ Current liabilities
Cash flow interest coverage.	Ability of operating cash flows to meet company fixed charge obligation	Operating cash Flows + interest/ interest charges

Ratios analysis only tends to be useful when we can observe a trend or we can compare it to a standard or benchmark. The absolute values have little meaning. As discussed before, to observe a trend, you need to analyze three to five years of historical data, or you could use a benchmark such as an industry average.

In conclusion, analysis of the cash flows of a company helps us analyze the efficiency and effectiveness of the company's uses of cash flow. It helps the management to look at cash flow from an operational perspective, rather than considering it simply as part of the finance function. This also helps the management to gain greater insights and then uses that information to strategize for the company's growth.

KEY BUSINESS QUESTIONS

Current state

The answers to the following questions will allow you to analyze the current state of control over cash flows in your company and might offer precious insights about ways to boost your cash flow.

- ✓ Do you have a cash flow reporting system in place?
- ✓ Do you forecast future cash flows?
- ✓ Do you analyze cash flows and take remedial actions if needed?
- ✓ Is the operating cash your primary source of cash inflows?
- ✓ Does your company have optimum levels of leverage?

Six months from now

The answers to these questions will help you to gauge your progress in the past six months and will point out the most effective strategies.

- ✓ Were you able to put a monthly cash flow reporting system in place? What were the challenges?
- ✓ Were you able to set up a system to forecast future cash flows?
- ✓ Did you set up a process to analyze cash flows and take remedial actions if needed?
- ✓ Is the operating cash your primary source of cash inflows?
- ✓ Does your company have optimum levels of leverage?

Twelve months from now

The answers to these questions will help you to gauge your progress in the past 12 months.

- ✓ Were you able to overcome the challenges in putting a monthly cash flow reporting system in place?
- ✓ Did you create a process for making sales forecasts and cash plans?
- ✓ Do you plan to monitor the plan's performance with respect to the plan?
- ✓ Was there considerable difference between the planned and actual result in the past 12 months?
- ✓ Are you able to identify the reasons for these differences?
- ✓ What benefits did you notice by having regular reporting and controls over cash flow?
- ✓ How much has the cash flow improved in the past 12 months? What strategies have contributed most to the improvement?

Free Cash Flow and Business Value Creation

In this book, we understood the importance of cash flow management and its impact on a company's overall performance. We were also introduced to the concept of free cash flow. In this chapter, we will discuss and understand in detail the importance of **free cash flow (FCF)** and its impact on the overall business's value, also known as enterprise value.

After reading this chapter, you will be able to:

- ✓ Understand the concept of free cash flow and business value
- ✓ Understand how free cash flow impacts the business's value
- ✓ Calculate the enterprise value of your business

Warren Buffet rightly equates free cash flow to "owner's earnings." For small businesses, free cash flow (FCF) primarily gives us an idea of the amount of cash available for the business owners, or if the business has debt as well as equity, then it signifies the cash available for all kinds of security holders. This would include the owners who hold equity and the creditors, such as banks who have lent money to the business. For large companies, the security holders would include equity owners, debtors, convertible stockowners, preferred shares owners, etc.

Enterprise value, business value, or firm value is the metric that reflects the market value of the complete business. It is primarily the sum of all the claims that are owed by the business, which would include the debtors as well as equity holders. The enterprise value gives us an idea of the value of a company's ongoing operations. Theoretically it could be considered the buying price for a company free of its obligations such as debt and other liabilities.

To measure a business's value, the enterprise value could be used in lieu of market capitalization. Traditionally, market capitalization has also been used as an indicator of a company's worth; however, enterprise value is a more accurate metric as it considers equity as well as debt. Hence, it is a more accurate metric for calculating the buying price of the company as well.

All the decisions that a small business owner makes will have an impact on the business's value in some form or the other. It would impact the company's current worth as well as its worth in the future. Despite the fact that you have built your business from scratch or have taken the ownership from a previous owner, you must continually challenge and question yourself about how you are creating and enhancing the business's value.

Understanding business value and wealth

Economically speaking, a business's value is created when the business is able to generate revenue, which is well above the economic costs required to generate it. Costs could primarily be divided into four sources: payrolls and benefits; raw materials and supplies, depreciation of assets; corporate income taxes and other taxes; and the opportunity cost of the capital. (Opportunity cost is generally referred to as the cost of capital. However, it is an opportunity cost as it represents the return that has been foregone on an alternate investment opportunity of similar risk.)

If we consider the value-based view that a business's value is created when revenues exceed all costs, the total cost that also includes a capital charge, this value would accrue to the residual owners of the firm. Business owners need to generate value, which exceeds the costs of resources utilized, inclusive of the cost of capital. The reason is that if you have invested in your business, then, most of the time, the aim is to make more money; hence, you expect a fair return to compensate for the risk you are taking. Ideally a business's value should be more than the opportunity cost of the invested capital.

Wealth creation in this case would refer to the change in the wealth of business owners or equity holders on a periodic basis (mostly considered on an annual basis). For public companies, the change in shareholder wealth is deduced from changes in stock prices, or from the dividends paid during the period.

Although there could be a difference in the theoretical business value and shareholder wealth for publically listed firms, for small privately owned businesses, the term is generally used interchangeably.

Relating free cash flows to market values

A firm's enterprise value or market value is usually the investor's/buyer's or equity holder's expectations of future cash flows. If the business is able to generate the expected cash flows or the future expectations from it remain constant, the business value is also likely to remain constant. If the company's cash flows turn out to be better than expected, market value is likely to rise; if cash flows or the cash flow expectations decline, the business's value is likely to erode.

In this section, we will learn how the FCF relates to the enterprise value. We can see that the owner's profit at the end of each year is derived from the FCF, as it is the cash flow after making all the necessary capital expenditures for future growth. Now, a business's value would be the NPV of the business's potential to create wealth for the owner; hence, it would be the NPV of the expected future free cash flows and the present value (PV) of the company's terminal value. The flow chart below shows the steps to calculate the enterprise value:

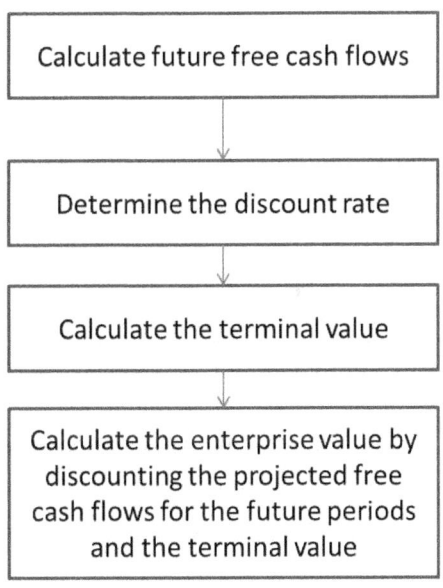

Let us discuss these steps in detail:

Calculate future free cash flows:

Use the projected financial statements to calculate the future free cash flows.

	Operating Profit
−	Adjusted Taxes
=	**Net Operating Profit After Taxes (NOPAT)**
+	Depreciation
+/−	Working Capital
−	Capital Expenditures
=	**Free Cash Flows (FCF)**

Determine the discount rate:

The general practice is to use the weighted average cost of capital (WACC), that is, the weighted average of the cost of debt and equity.

Calculate the terminal value:

$$\text{Terminal value} = FCF/(WACC - \text{Growth rate})$$

This formula holds true when we assume that the company would grow perpetually at the same growth rate.

Calculate enterprise value:

> **Enterprise value** = PV of FCFs + PV of terminal value

This represents today's enterprise value or the business value of the company as of today.

Managing for free cash flows and value creation for the business owner

For any business, the fundamental reason for its existence is to enhance the shareholder's value or we can say the business owner's wealth for small businesses. This requires an increase in the NPV of the future stream of free cash flows. There are three primary ways to achieve this goal:

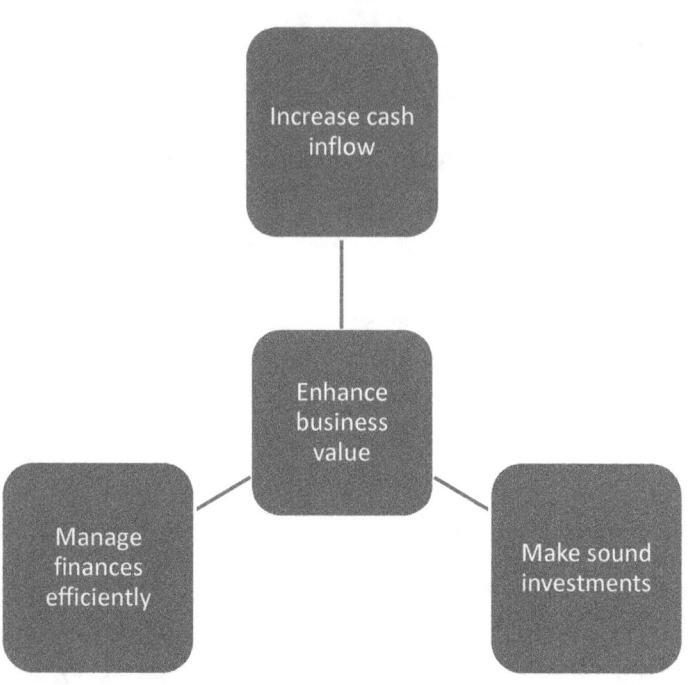

1. <u>Increase cash inflows</u>: This is achieved by growing the business sustainably. We have discussed numerous strategies in the previous chapters to enhance your cash inflows and, hence, cash earnings. Growing the free cash flows is more important than growing the business in an unsustainable manner or simply focusing on profitability, as an increase in profits may or may not be equivalent to an increase in the free cash flows. It's essential that growth could enhance the free cash flows after taking into account additional investments needed in working capital and assets as and when required, to support the growth.

2. <u>Making sound investments</u>: This means managing working capital and capital expenditure tightly and doing sound analysis before making an investment decision. A cost benefit analysis could help you ascertain the future benefit potential of an investment.

3. <u>Managing finances efficiently:</u> This includes keeping the company's cost of capital in check. Often, this could mean increasing the debt portion of the capital, as it is usually cheaper than raising equity. This also includes managing cash shortfalls and efficient investment of excess cash. The most important financial management challenge for any company is to use free cash flows efficiently to invest in new opportunities that further enhance the business's value. Every investment made by a company, whether it is equipment, a new warehouse, or the acquisition of a competitor should be valuated properly and the decision should be made on future benefits.

In conclusion, we understand that for any business the primary purpose is to build or enhance the equity holder's wealth, which is directly dependent on the company's FCF. The business owner could also take out a profit for himself at the year-end from the FCF, without impacting on the workings of the future growth of the business. Hence, FCF growth is important for wealth generation of the business owner.

The FCF is, in turn, dependent on the company's overall cash flow; hence, it should be the primary objective of any business to encourage policies and practices that contribute in enhancing the cash flow. By following the strategies for cash management mentioned in this book, you are likely to achieve your company growth objectives as well as build wealth for yourself.

Doing Nothing is Unacceptable

Thank you for staying true to yourself and finishing to this last part of the book. Now is the time to take massive action. If you are one that keeps wondering where the money is going and not seem to have any money left, even though your business is making a profit, now is the time to pause and use the knowledge you have gained from this book and apply them.

Many business owners do not understand finances and it is not their fault. They are set to do business based on what technical skills they are good at. Unless your business is happened to be in banking, money lending and services related closely to financial products. Most of the business owners are not an expert in financial.

We must take note that nothing will change unless we doing something different. Changes do not happen overnight. It takes time and effort. But however, success will always follow when conscious efforts are being applied.

Are *you* going to do something about it today?

There are only three choices.

1) Best choice.

2) Good choice.

3) Worst choice.

You would know that the best choice gives you a result that is far better than your expectations. Good choice is when the result meets your expectation. Finally is the worst choice, which is *doing nothing*. You do not want to be in the worst choice.

GO FOR THE BEST CHOICE TODAY

About the Author

Mok Tuck Sung is a seasoned entrepreneur, business owner, coach, trainer, and cash flow turnaround specialist for more than a decade. Some of Mok's accomplishments are as follows:

1) Turning around businesses from distress in less than 60 days.
2) Turning around businesses and doubling their sales sustainably in 18 months.
3) Turning around businesses and increasing their cash flow by 35%.
4) Turning around businesses and restructuring them into manageable and profitable enterprises.
5) Coaching business owners in meeting their cash flow objectives.
6) Coaching start-ups to become more strategically positioned to compete in the market.
7) Conducting hands-on workshops for serious business owners who want to better their cash flow.
8) Providing retainer business coaching service for serious business owners who know that even Tiger Woods needs a coach.
9) Pro bono turnaround service for social enterprise and for-profit businesses.

Mok holds a BBus, MBA, and an Advanced Certificate in Training and Assessment.

--END--

www.ingramcontent.com/pod-product-compliance
Lightning Source LLC
Chambersburg PA
CBHW051705170526
45167CB00002B/545